Q 149 .U5 B57 1989

Blacks, science, and
American education

W9-AAF-371

DATE DUE

JUL 9 2001

GAYLORD   PRINTED IN U.S.A.

BLACKS, SCIENCE,

AND AMERICAN EDUCATION

BLACKS, SCIENCE,

AND AMERICAN

EDUCATION

Edited by
WILLIE PEARSON, JR., and
H. KENNETH BECHTEL

RUTGERS UNIVERSITY PRESS
New Brunswick and London

Copyright © 1989 by Rutgers, The State University
All Rights Reserved
Manufactured in the United States of America

Library of Congress Cataloging-in-Publication Data

Blacks, science, and American education.

  Bibliography: p.
  Includes index.
  1. Afro-American scientists—United States.
  2. Afro-Americans—Education—United States—Science.
  3. Science—Study and teaching—United States.
  I. Pearson, Willie, 1945–   II. Bechtel,
  H. Kenneth, 1946–
  Q149.U5B57   1989   508′.996′073   88-30606
  ISBN 0-8135-1397-9

British Cataloging-in-Publication information available

To

SHIRLEY M. MALCOM

CONTENTS

List of Figures ix

List of Tables xi

WALTER E. MASSEY

Foreword xiii

Preface xv

Acknowledgments xvii

Contributors xix

H. KENNETH BECHTEL

Introduction 1

I. Student Participation

JOSEPHINE D. DAVIS

1. The Mathematics Education of Black High School Students 23

BERNICE ANDERSON

2. Black Participation and Performance in High School Science 43

GAIL E. THOMAS

3. Black Science Majors in Colleges and Universities 59

ALAN FECHTER

4. A Statistical Portrait of Black Ph.D.s 79

II. Strategies for Increased Participation

BEATRIZ C. CLEWELL

5. Intervention Programs: Three Case Studies 105

JERRY GASTON

6. The Benefits of Black Participation in Science 123

WILLIE PEARSON, JR.

7. The Future of Blacks in Science: Summary and Recommendations 137

Bibliography 153

Index 167

FIGURES

1.1. Mathematics Course Enrollment Pattern   31
1.2. Performance on Total Test   33
1.3. The Davis Achievement Model   39
4.1. Distribution of Black Ph.D.s   81
4.2. Percentage Distribution of Newly Awarded Black Ph.D.s   83
4.3. Employment Trends by Selected Sectors   87
4.4 Employment Trends by Selected Work Activities   92
4.5. Median Salaries of Black and White Ph.D.s   98
4.6. Salaries of Black Ph.D.s   99

TABLES

I.1. Public School Expenditures 6
1.1. Sᴀᴛ-Mathematics Scores for College-Bound Seniors 26
1.2. Math Performance Levels 27
1.3. Academic Tracking 30
1.4. Secondary Mathematics Course Enrollment 30
1.5. Mathematics Achievement 34
1.6. Within-Group Comparisons of Mathematics Achievement 35
1.7. Report of Classroom Experiences 36
2.1. Positive Responses to Attitudinal Items 46
2.2. Years of Science Study 50
2.3. Science Exposure, Attitudes, and Achievement 52
3.1. Enrollments in Undergraduate and Graduate Institutions 65
3.2. Bachelors', Masters', and Doctors' Degrees Awarded 66
3.3. The Role of Institutions in Awarding Degrees 70
3.4. Bachelors' Degrees Awarded to Blacks 72
3.5. Masters' Degrees Awarded to Blacks 73
3.6. Doctors' Degrees Awarded to Blacks 74
4.1. Black Ph.D.s by Broad Field 80
4.2. Black Ph.D.s by Broad Field and Sex 82
4.3. Sources of Support for Ph.D. Training 84
4.4. Postgraduate Plans of New Ph.D.s 85
4.5. Underutilization Rates for Ph.D.s 86
4.6. Underutilization Rates of Ph.D.s in the Total Work Force 86
4.7. Ph.D.s by Field and Sector of Employment 88
4.8. Science Ph.D.s by Field and Primary Work Activity 91
4.9. Academically Employed, Tenured Ph.D.s 94
4.10. Faculty Ph.D.s by Field 95
4.11. Distribution of Ph.D. Faculty (1985) 96
4.12. Distribution of Ph.D. Faculty (1975 and 1985) 97
6.1. Distribution of Scientists Employed in Science 127
6.2. Social Origins of University Faculty by Academic Field 128
6.3. Degree and Work Specialties of Chemists 129

FOREWORD

Even rarer than black scientists are good books about black scientists, especially books that help us to understand why there are so few blacks in science and that also suggest practical programs for improving the situation in the future.

This book, *Blacks, Science, and American Education,* does both these things and more. The combination of analytical data, policy recommendations, and narratives describing the personal struggles and achievements of some of our most noteworthy black scientists makes this book unique. It is a valuable resource for anyone wishing to understand the background and contribute to the goal of increasing the number of blacks in science and other technical fields. For these reasons alone, I would have been very proud to write this foreword.

What makes me even more proud, however, is that the book is dedicated to Dr. Shirley Malcom. Few individuals in the United States have done more over the past decade to develop, support, and disseminate programs and information that can help blacks and other minorities enter scientific and technical fields. In her role as program head of the American Association for the Advancement of Science (AAAS) Office of Opportunities in Science, she has been instrumental in leading national efforts to increase the number of presently underrepresented groups in science and technology. The programs she has helped to initiate address the needs of the handicapped and women, as well as racial and ethnic minorities, in a practical and consistent manner.

Shirley Malcom's education and development as a scientist serve as object lessons for many of the points made in this book. Born in Birmingham, Alabama, she finished George Washington Carver High School in that city in 1963. She has said it was quite an experience going from Carver High School to the predominantly white University of Washington in Seattle, where she was usually the only black in her science classes, many times the only woman, and always the only black woman.

Malcom has said that her life has consisted of a series of twists and turns due to serendipitous circumstances. She had initially intended to become a doctor, because she was unaware that there were other careers for a young, black woman interested in science. A professor at the University of Washington, whom she calls her first mentor, recognized her interest in and ability to do research and encouraged her to enter graduate school in the biological sciences. After obtaining a master's degree at UCLA and teaching high school for two years in California, she returned home to Birmingham, and at that time had no plans to pursue a doctorate degree.

However, her ambition could not be contained for long, and she reentered graduate school at Penn State University, this time with the goal of obtaining a (nonresearch) doctor of arts degree in teaching. Again, her talent and interest were recognized, and a professor at Penn State encouraged her to do research with him to obtain a Ph.D. degree in biology. Another fortuitous circumstance at Penn State occurred when she met her husband while standing in line to register for classes. It happened that both their names began with the letters "Ma."

Her interest in developing programs to increase the number of minorities in the sciences grew out of her attempts to develop ways for minorities to become research scientists without having to depend on chance circumstances. One of her accomplishments has been to help others find and follow those more rational and systematic ways toward careers in science.

Shirley Malcom's career is a vivid reminder of the importance of mentors in the development of young scholars. Her achievements also remind those of us who are practicing professional scientists and teachers of the obligation we owe to the next generation to act as mentors and role models ourselves. Having been a high school teacher, college professor, government administrator, and now a distinguished member of the science policy community, Shirley Malcom is indeed a role model for us all.

WALTER E. MASSEY
August 1988

PREFACE

The fact that blacks are significantly underrepresented in American science and mathematics is well known and commonly acknowledged. Most scholars of American science neglect to include blacks as subjects in their investigations; frequently, their exclusion of blacks is justified by blacks' marginal participation in science and mathematics.

For the first time, significant and rich data are available on a large group of prospective black professional scientists and mathematicians. These unique data sources provide an opportunity to examine the flow of black students through the educational pipeline and, ultimately, into the workplace. These data sources (even with their limitations) should help identify those factors which inhibit the free participation of blacks in the scientific community. This book marks the first chance for a number of nationally recognized researchers to present their analyses and policy recommendations under one cover for a wide public.

The book is designed to raise general historical and sociological questions, to provide the best and most up-to-date statistical data, and to propose solutions to a real problem. In the Introduction, H. Kenneth Bechtel's sociohistorical overview links the issues of race, limited opportunities, and the structure of science. Among the questions addressed are, How have social, political, and legal policies inhibited the full participation of gifted blacks in American science? In the face of such difficulties, what contributions have blacks made to American science? How has their work been recognized and rewarded by their peers in the scientific community?

The limited participation of blacks in science begins early in their lives. In Chapters 1 and 2, Josephine D. Davis and Bernice Anderson look at the experiences of black students in and out of high school math and science classes. Anderson's data from NAEP gives a clear picture of the present status of blacks in science through the presentation of enrollment, attitudinal, and achievement data in science for black high school students. The data are examined to document changes in science achievement and to compare the science achievements and experiences of black high school students to high school students nationally. Josephine Davis's points about curricular reform in math apply equally well to the sciences, stressing that if the problem of the black experience in mathematics were more clearly understood, policymakers would be able to make more efficient decisions regarding resource allocation. She then identifies some of the key variables associated with the opportunity black students have to learn mathematics and the effect these variables have on achievement.

Chapters 3 and 4 explore the current situation of blacks in science beyond high school—primarily their college and postcollege experiences. Using the most recent reliable data from the Office of Civil Rights survey on black student higher education enrollment and degree completion in the natural and technical sciences, Gail E. Thomas, in Chapter 3, assesses the progress of blacks in these fields relative to whites. She also presents data to determine the extent to which various colleges and universities have been productive in enrolling and graduating black undergraduate and graduate students in selected majors in the natural and technical sciences. In Chapter 4, Alan Fechter examines black doctorates in science fields and generates a statistical portrait of their career participation and development in these fields. Fechter bases his findings on the most currently available data (1975–1985) generated by two surveys of the doctorate population: 1) the Survey of Doctorate Recipients, a biennial longitudinal survey of a sample of doctorate holders, and 2) the Survey of Earned Doctorates, an annual survey of new doctoral degree recipients.

Part II considers the possible impact of increased minority representation in science and the strategies for bringing this about. Chapter 5 presents the findings of case studies done by Beatriz C. Clewell describing three intervention programs that serve primarily black students. Each intervention program was targeted at a different point along the educational pipeline: junior high, high school, and undergraduate freshmen and sophomores. These data are presented to support the claims that intervention efforts aimed at pre–high school and high school students will address the problems contributing to low black participation in math and science. Jerry Gaston presents an essay in Chapter 6 in which he argues that science would benefit if more blacks were recruited. The basis for his argument is evidence suggesting that social processes affect who becomes scientists, what kind of scientists they become, and what specialties they choose. If problem choice is influenced by the same social processes, then Gaston claims it is desirable to recruit scientists from all social categories in order to maximize the probability that particular research problems are not neglected.

The unique value of these studies is that they draw on diverse sources, lead to significant conclusions, and form the basis for establishing policy in science and mathematics education for the future. These issues are specifically addressed in Chapter 7, where Willie Pearson, Jr, draws together the substantive conclusions suggested by the findings of the contributors to this volume. Based on his review, Pearson then makes recommendations on the future directions of science policy and research with regard to black participation in the American scientific community.

W. P., JR.
H. K. B.
Winston-Salem, North Carolina
November 1988

ACKNOWLEDGMENTS

Completion of this book required the help of many individuals whose contributions, both great and small, were of immense importance. First and foremost, we owe a special debt of gratitude to the contributors who provided the most important ingredient: their ideas and research findings that make this book what it is. Without individuals willing to write original chapters and put up with constant harassment from the editors, a book of this type would be impossible to undertake, let alone complete.

We owe special thanks to our editorial review board, which includes Robert D. Bullard, University of California–Berkeley; John R. Earle, Wake Forest University; Herman E. Eure, Wake Forest University; Eleanor Hall, Life Insurance Marketing and Research Association (LIMRA) International; Shirley M. Malcom, American Association for the Advancement of Science; Regina McNeil, A. C. Nielsen; Donald Powers, Educational Testing Service; Earl Smith, Washington State University; William T. Trent, University of Illinois–Urbana/Champaign; Isiah M. Warner, Emory University; John S. Wilson, Jr., Massachusetts Institute of Technology; Herman A. Young, University of Louisville; Gwendolyn L. Lewis, The College Board; and Daryl E. Chubin, Office of Technology Assessment. Their careful reading of initial drafts was enormously helpful to the editors and contributors alike.

A special mention of appreciation goes to Karen Reeds, Science Editor at Rutgers University Press, for her encouragement, support, and expert critiques during the inception and throughout the completion of this book. In addition to Karen, we would like to thank the anonymous reviewers for taking their time to review our manuscript and for providing insightful suggestions for improving the final product. The willingness of scholars to offer their valuable time to help others too often goes unrecognized and unappreciated.

Among our colleagues at Wake Forest, we are especially indebted to Phil Perricone for his administrative support. We also appreciate the able assistance of our former departmental secretary, the late Arlene Casey, for many hours of typing and technical help.

As prepublication readers, LaRue Cunningham Pearson, Darlene Weiss Bechtel, Johnsie Cunningham Bullock, and Prattsie Cunningham-Brown provided useful criticism and editorial assistance.

Several Wake Forest University undergraduate assistants contributed to the final product. We want to thank Connie Phillips, Jennifer Plybon, Heather Scull, Karen Baynes, and Jacqueline Williamson for their many hours of clerical and technical assistance.

This publication was made possible in part by a grant from the Wake Forest University Research and Publication Fund. We are especially grateful to

Provost Edwin G. Wilson and Dean Thomas E. Mullen at Wake Forest University for their administrative support.

Finally, we thank our wives, LaRue and Darlene, for providing encouragement and a supportive environment throughout the duration of this project. We, of course, take all responsibility for any deficiencies in the final product.

CONTRIBUTORS

WILLIE PEARSON, JR., is professor of sociology at Wake Forest University in Winston-Salem, North Carolina. His main fields of interest are the sociology of science and of the family. He has published in various scholarly journals and is the author of *Black Scientists, White Society, and Colorless Science* (1985). He received his doctorate from Southern Illinois University–Carbondale in 1981 and is currently a Congressional Fellow with the Office of Technology Assessment in Washington, D.C.

H. KENNETH BECHTEL is an assistant professor of sociology at Wake Forest University, Winston-Salem, North Carolina. He received his doctorate in sociology from Southern Illinois University–Carbondale in 1983 and has conducted research and published in the areas of deviance in science and the historical presence of minorities in science. Currently he is investigating the life of Edward Alexander Bouchet, the first black to receive a doctorate from an American university.

BERNICE T. ANDERSON is an associate research scientist in the Education Policy Research and Service Division at Educational Testing Service, Princeton, New Jersey. Her work at ETS has focused largely on minority-related research issues. Currently she is conducting research on unsuccessful black medical-school applicants, science interests of young minority and female students, and intervention programs in mathematics and science for middle school minority and female students. Her doctorate is from Rutgers University, and her undergraduate degree is from Norfolk State University.

BEATRIZ C. CLEWELL is a research scientist in the Education Policy Research and Service Division at Educational Testing Service, Princeton, New Jersey. She received her doctorate from Florida State University in 1980. She has directed research and published articles relating to minority access to and retention in undergraduate, graduate, and professional education. She recently was co-director of a project to determine characteristics and experiences of high-achieving Hispanic students. She is presently director of an effort to identify intervention programs in math, science, and computer science for minority and female students in grades four through eight.

JOSEPHINE D. DAVIS, professor of mathematics and dean of the Graduate School, Albany State College, was a 1985–1986 Visiting Scholar at the National Assessment of Educational Progress Center, Princeton, New Jersey. Her primary research emphasis is the teaching and learning of mathematics, focusing on racial and ethnic minorities. She is a member of the National

Science Foundation's Committee on Equal Opportunities in Science and Engineering. She received a bachelor's degree from Spelman College, a master's degree from the University of Notre Dame, and a doctorate in education from Rutgers University. She was recently selected as a Kellogg Fellow.

ALAN FECHTER is the executive director of the Office of Scientific and Engineering Personnel at the National Research Council. In 1972 he became senior research associate with the Urban Institute. In 1978 he accepted a position at the National Science Foundation, where he was head of the Scientific and Technical Personnel Studies Section, Division of Science Resources Studies. During his tenure he confronted such topics as the expected impact of the current defense buildup on scientific and technical personnel, the quality of the scientific and technical work force, and the role of women and minorities in this work force. He has been affiliated with the National Research Council since 1983.

JERRY GASTON is associate provost and professor of sociology at Texas A. and M. University. He is a sociologist of science who focuses primarily on issues related to reward systems in science. He received his doctorate in 1969 from Yale University and has chaired the sociology departments at Southern Illinois University–Carbondale and Texas A. and M. University. His essays have appeared in such journals as *American Sociological Review, British Journal of Sociology,* and *New Scientist.* He is the author of *Originality and Competition in Science* (1973), *The Reward System in British and American Science* (1978), the editor of *The Sociology of Science* (1978), and the co-editor (with R. K. Merton) of *The Sociology of Science in Europe* (1977).

GAIL E. THOMAS is professor of sociology at Texas A. and M. University, having served previously as principal research scientist at Johns Hopkins University. She received her doctoral degree from the University of North Carolina–Chapel Hill. Thomas has written a variety of articles and monographs on the achievement of minorities and women in undergraduate and graduate education. She edited *Black Students in Higher Education* (1981) and authored a recent *Harvard Education Review* article, "Black Students in U.S. Graduate and Professional Schools in the 1980s: A National Assessment" (September 1987).

BLACKS, SCIENCE,

AND AMERICAN EDUCATION

H. KENNETH BECHTEL

Introduction

Science is a pervasive and dominating force in American society. It is a primary source of the understanding of the worlds—physical, biological, behavioral, and social—in which we live; directly or indirectly, it shapes the boundaries and directions of all phases of American life. As a major institutional component of our society, the scientific community inevitably reflects the values of American society at large in its own social structures, beliefs, and attitudes. And, like American society in general, American science reflects the dominance of whites. The black scientist in America is historically an anomaly and currently a statistical rarity. In 1984 blacks accounted for only 2.3 percent, or 90,500, of the 3,995,000 employed scientists and engineers (National Science Foundation 1986). Of scientists and engineers holding doctorates, only 1.3 percent are black (National Science Foundation 1986). Yet blacks now constitute 12 percent of the total population and 10 percent of the American work force. That striking underrepresentation of blacks in the scientific community demands our concern.

This volume documents statistically the current status of blacks in American science, examines the causes of this underrepresentation, and, above all, assesses the role of American education in training black scientists. In very simple terms, the source of the problem is obvious: There are few black scientists because there are few blacks in graduate science programs; there are few blacks in graduate programs because there are few blacks who are encouraged to take the undergraduate courses required for successful scientific careers; there are few black undergraduates who are prepared by their high schools or grade schools to choose such courses. And at every point along the pipeline to a scientific career, large numbers of the young black men and women who could be scientists turn away. Where does this happen? Why does it happen? And what can be done about it?

The shortage of blacks among the ranks of scientists, engineers, and mathematicians is not the result of some recent misdirected social policy. Rather, it is one dimension of the larger story of blacks in American society and needs to be understood by reviewing past ideologies, practices, policies, and expectations of whites and blacks. It is necessary to examine the sociohistorical links among attitudes about race, educational policies, and the social structure of science. All three have worked to prevent blacks from entering science or from having their scientific contributions acknowledged and rewarded.

Education of Blacks

For most of the history of the United States, educational policies toward blacks were generally designed with one goal in mind: to ensure the political, social, economic, and intellectual inferiority of blacks. The policies worked well, and even after America began to revoke them, their legacy remains the major cause of the educational deprivation and retardation of blacks.

During the first half-century of the nation's history, in New England and the mid-Atlantic states specifically, revolutionary spirit, growing abolitionist sentiment, and Christian missionary fervor favored the education of blacks. The work of various religious groups, most notably the Quakers, to establish schools for blacks is well documented. The efforts to provide instruction to blacks during this period were generally local and unconnected, reflecting the interests of the diverse groups involved. Thus, some communities provided integrated public instruction while others had separate facilities. The growing intensity of antislavery sentiments in parts of the North prompted some communities to adopt policies that would allow more blacks to attend public schools (Woodson 1915; Frazier 1949; Franklin 1973).

The results of this movement were impressive as free blacks took advantage of opportunities to get an education. Of the 2,000 blacks in Boston in 1850, almost 1,500 were in school; and in the states and territories as a whole, 32,629 blacks were in school in 1860. Blacks also began to move into higher education: in 1826 Edward Jones graduated from Amherst while John Russwurm was getting his degree from Bowdoin—the first blacks to graduate from college in America. Blacks were attending Oberlin and other institutions of higher education well before the Civil War (Franklin 1973; Pifer 1973).

Although most of these educational efforts were provided and controlled by whites, blacks also played a role. A few schools were established by blacks, and in such large cities as Philadelphia blacks began to organize literary societies as early as the 1780s (Funke 1920; Winston 1971).

The social climate in the South during the slavery era effectively precluded educating blacks. Interest in public education in general was low. Whites who wanted schooling were expected to rely on their families for financial support. There were a few isolated efforts to provide free blacks with an education, and some progressive plantation owners felt morally bound to teach their slaves to read and write. Any possibility of these practices gaining widespread support quickly vanished with the abortive revolts by Prosser (1800) and Vesey (1822), and the Turner rebellion (1831). These actions by blacks who had been educated so frightened the planters that laws were passed throughout the South making it illegal to instruct any slave or free black (Funke 1920; Franklin 1973; Low and Clift 1981).

During the decade of Reconstruction following the Civil War, blacks made temporary gains in their social and political conditions. Passage of the Thirteenth, Fourteenth, and Fifteenth amendments to the Constitution and the Civil Rights Act of 1866 gave blacks freedom and rights of citizenship and hindered restrictive legislation that attempted to reestablish antebellum social relationships (Bond 1969; Brawley 1970). Probably the most significant change came in the area of education. The emancipated slaves were eager to take advantage of their new status and felt that getting an education was of primary importance. And many individuals and organizations interested in aiding the freedmen were quick to offer their services (Woodson 1969).

Even before the war ended, missionaries began to make their way into the Southern states to establish educational programs for those blacks freed by the advancing Union troops. Immediately after the war, religious organizations, such as the American Missionary Association and the government-sponsored Freedmen's Bureau, established schools in the South. Blacks responded eagerly, and thousands were attending schools by the late 1860s (Funke 1920; Bond 1934; Cruden 1969).

White Southerners, however, were unprepared for such a radical change and opposed efforts to provide education for blacks, who were considered innately inferior—the idea of educating them was viewed as absurd. Providing educational opportunities to blacks would have meant extending a privilege that had historically been restricted to the upper classes in the South; it would elevate the former slave to a status higher than that of most former slave owners. Conservative Southerners feared that the schools taught by Northerners would instill Republican ideals of equality and further undermine their political power. The hostile reaction by Southerners to black education was a predictable part of their attempt to maintain the traditional antebellum social order in the face of massive social dislocation.

Nevertheless, some Southern whites grasped an obvious fact: the freedmen would have to be educated simply to survive and provide for their own basic needs. At the end of the Civil War, 95 percent of the black population in America was illiterate. To most enlightened observers, the presence of this large number of "ignorant black rabble was a menacing Trojan horse"

(Winston 1971, 681). White Southerners faced a serious dilemma that went beyond simple questions of educational philosophy. The way this problem was addressed would have a significant impact on important issues of political and economic relationships, because once whites chose to educate blacks, they had to decide what type of education should be provided. And that decision ultimately depended upon the role that whites saw for blacks in the American social order.

From an egalitarian perspective, education is a means of raising those less fortunate up to a level on par with the rest of society. If such a goal had been paramount at the end of the Civil War, what sort of educational program could have been developed? Allen Ballard (1973, 11) describes a possible scenario.

> First, there would have to be federally funded elementary schools in every village. Second, a federally funded group of highly trained teachers would have been sent to those villages. Centers of literacy would have to be established for adult education. This first thrust could have carried through for five to ten years, to be followed by the establishment of regional high schools with both vocational and academic curricula to serve as the funnel through which the most able black youth would have gone on to federally subsidized colleges. Over a period of fifty or seventy-five years the educational level of the Africans would have risen to that of white Americans.

Ballard makes clear that it was unthinkable that whites during Reconstruction would have allowed anything of the sort. If blacks had to be educated, white Southerners felt, let that education be suited to their inferior mental capacities and to their proper, subservient place in society. With the goal decided upon, the two pillars of post-Reconstruction black educational philosophy emerged: a system of separate and unequal schools for blacks, and industrial education.

During Reconstruction, the quality of education provided in the South had been generally poor for both blacks and whites, but it was administered on a fairly equal basis. After the end of Reconstruction and the reemergence of Southern conservatives in political power, the policies of black social and political disenfranchisement extended to black education as well. Through deception, blatant discrimination, and law, white schools were improved at the expense of black schools. An examination of the data on school expenditures from the mid-1870s to 1930 clearly reveals the massive disparities between the education of whites and blacks in the South.

Data (Bond 1934, 153) for the state of Alabama indicate the changes that took place over the fifty-five-year period from 1875 to 1930. During the 1875/1876 school term, Alabama spent an average of $1.30 per pupil for white teachers' salaries and $1.46 per pupil for black teachers' salaries. This difference in favor of blacks reflects the impact of the Reconstruction administration. By 1885, however, Alabama was paying black teachers 85 percent of what was paid to white teachers ($1.09 versus $1.28). And twenty-five years later, black Alabama teachers still received only $1.10 per pupil while their white counterparts got nearly six times as much ($6.42).

While the figures from Alabama show the dramatic decline over time in expenditures to black teachers, the data from Tennessee reveal no change whatsoever over the sixty-year period from 1870 to 1930. In 1870 Tennessee paid its white teachers $11.83 per pupil compared to $7.48 for black teachers—63 percent of the white teachers' salary. By 1931 Tennessee was paying its white teachers $27.55 per pupil compared to $17.25 for black teachers—again only 63 percent of the white teachers' salary (Bond 1934, 158–159).

Harlan (1968, 38) noted that the regional differences in funding for white schools paled when compared to the economic disadvantages suffered by black schools. In 1915 the North Central states spent an average of $28.00 per white child for education compared to only $14.00 per white child in South Carolina. But at the same time, South Carolina was spending only $1.13 per black child for education.

The data presented in Table I.1 reveal the degree of inferiority of funding of black education compared to that of whites in the South. Using Washington, D.C., as a point of comparison, one finds that spending by the six Southern states on school expenses, school property, and teacher salaries falls far short of anything that could be remotely called "equal" education. The breadth of the discrimination against black education is revealed in other areas as well. For example, during the 1933/1934 school year, ten Southern states spent a total of $20 million on transporting rural school children. But, only 3 percent of this money was spent on black children who constituted 34 percent of the total school population. In 1935/1936 over half (55 percent) of the 24,405 black public elementary schools in the eighteen states with separate schools were one-room schools. In terms of total property value, in ten Southern states for which data were available, for every $1.00 invested in school property for each white student, only $0.19 was invested for each black student (Frazier 1949, 434–435).

Factors other than direct discrimination in finances also undermined the ability of blacks to acquire an adequate education. Black attendance remained relatively low because black schools were often distant and so little transportation was provided. But because the number of black teachers was also small, the typical teacher in a black school would, on the average, have twice as many students as the typical teacher in a white school (see Table Intro. 1). Possibly most damaging was the practice of having shorter terms for the black schools. In the 1929/1930 school year, for example, the average length of the term for the eighteen Southern and border states, including Washington, was

TABLE I.1. Public School Expenditures

	Average exp. per pupil		Black % exp.	Black % pop.	Average value of school property per pupil		Average annual teacher salary		Pupils per teacher	
	W	B			W	B	W	B	W	B
D.C.	$112.79	$96.31	26.0	25.2	$289.33	$237.23	$2,229	$2,099	29	32
Alabama	37.00	7.16	10.1	38.4	86.36	15.40	832	354	33	48
Georgia	31.52	6.98	14.0	41.7	73.34	11.01	768	260	34	46
Louisiana	40.64	7.84	12.1	38.9	140.68	18.53	1,159	496	30	53
Mississippi	31.33	5.94	20.0	52.2	93.94	17.50	908	350	30	53
S.C.	52.89	5.20	10.3	51.4	125.00	14.10	1,047	316	28	51
Virginia	47.46	13.30	11.0	29.9	111.03	38.28	902	502	31	40

SOURCE: Work 1931, 204–207.
NOTE: Selected data for six Southern states and the District of Columbia, 1930–1931.

164 days for whites and 144 days for blacks. However, in South Carolina the average school term was 173 days for whites compared to only 114 days for blacks (Work 1931, 205). After eight years of school, the typical black student in South Carolina would have been in class 472 days less than the typical white student—in other words, he or she would be approximately four years behind. This policy, combined with the fact that few secondary schools were established for blacks, goes far toward explaining why few blacks during this period attained more than a sixth-grade education (Rice 1971).

Much of this discussion of black education has focused on the Southern states. One must not conclude that the educational experiences of blacks in the North were any better. During the eighteenth and nineteenth centuries, blacks were few in number in the North and West and did not arouse the fear and apprehension found in the South. Life was therefore different for those blacks who lived in the various Northern states. They were not subject to the whims of a master; the restrictions on their activities were less severe; they could protest against injustices; and there were more opportunities for self-expression (such as churches and newspapers) and improvement in one's political and economic position (Quarles 1969; Litwack 1961).

Popular beliefs and attitudes about blacks were not restricted to a particular region of the country, and the belief in black inferiority was shared by most white Americans. Discrimination and racial segregation were facts of life for blacks North and South. And the justification for such practices was the same everywhere: blacks constituted an inferior race suited only for the most menial of positions (Litwack 1961).

Despite having comparatively greater freedom in the North, blacks found that there was strong opposition to their receiving an education. Many Northern states were unwilling to spend money on schools for blacks, fearing that more of them would move into their states or communities seeking education. Northerners seemed no more fond of blacks than Southerners. Ohio, Illinois, and Oregon had laws forbidding the migration of free blacks into their states. Although Northern states did not pass laws prohibiting the teaching of blacks, there was an undercurrent of resentment toward educating blacks that found expression in the forcible closing of schools, the intimidation and driving away of teachers, and the destruction of school buildings (Bond 1934; Beale 1975).

While some white schools in the North admitted blacks, this occurred mostly during the early 1800s. By 1830 most Northern states had excluded blacks from white schools and required them to attend separate all-black schools. Reflecting the prevailing belief in the limited intellectual capacity of blacks, these separate schools were often as unequal as those in the South, with substandard teachers, inadequate facilities, and inferior curricula (Litwack 1961).

Frazier (1949) has remarked that the problems facing blacks in the public schools of the North were similar to those faced by the large number of immigrants who settled in the major urban centers. As with the immigrants, blacks had been forced to live in the poorest sections of the cities and their children had to attend old, inferior, and overcrowded schools. Nevertheless, blacks suffered additional problems: because of their color, they were restricted in their movement both socially and economically. Greer (1973) notes that with varying degrees of speed, foreign immigrants were able to become part of American society, while blacks remained on the margin. Both groups were vulnerable because of their low social status, but it was the individual immigrant who suffered the consequences of economic change, while for blacks the entire group was affected. Thus, caste through race added a significant dimension to the life of the lower-class black in the urban North.

Despite widespread animosity toward blacks, they did receive more education in the North, although the quality of that education was inferior. Frazier (1949, 445–446) reports figures for 1940 that show the proportion of blacks with four years of high school in the South was only 25 percent of the total, while in the North it ranged from 50 to 75 percent of the total. The reality, however, is that North or South, blacks in America received an inadequate and inferior education when compared to that available for most whites.

The content of black schooling accurately reflected white goals for blacks in the social order. Industrial training was an effective way of ensuring that blacks could not rise beyond what was seen as their natural sphere as laborers and servants.

Industrial education had its beginnings at Hampton Institute under the direction of General Samuel Armstrong, a Freedmen's Bureau administrator in Hampton, Virginia. A believer in the innate inferiority of blacks, Armstrong thought that the best training for blacks was one that would instill self-control and provide a check on what he believed was the natural tendency of blacks toward rebellion. His program of education was intended to affect a change in the freedman's innately flawed character, to "civilize" the black by instilling "habits of living and labor" (Spivey 1978, 19). Armstrong believed that blacks were ultimately destined to "form the working classes" and remain at the bottom of the economic hierarchy (Spivey 1978, 22). Having no faith in blacks' intellectual capacity, Armstrong thought it was a waste of time to give them academic training, stating that courses involving "reading and elocution, geography and mathematics, history, the sciences . . . would, I think, make a curriculum that would exhaust the best powers of . . . those who would for years enter" Hampton (Spivey 1978, 26). Thus, education at Hampton under Armstrong was designed to maintain the Southern status quo. Black students would be trained in the principles of agriculture, unskilled menial labor, and domestic service—activities that would not be a threat to

white skilled workers and would keep blacks in their proper place in the social
and economic structure (Spivey 1978). But while Armstrong was the origina-
tor of vocational education, it took a black man to make industrial training a
prominent feature of black education.

Booker T. Washington was a student at Hampton and became convinced
that vocational education was the only means by which blacks would become
successful in America. In 1881 Washington went to Alabama and founded
Tuskegee Institute, where he put into practice his belief that the ultimate
solution to the race problem was for blacks to prove themselves worthy by
becoming reliable and superior laborers, eventually making themselves indis-
pensable to the economic well-being of the country. In order to accomplish
this, blacks must have the right form of education: an education that would be
beneficial in an economic sense. Given his experience at Hampton, Washington felt that industrial education was superior to academic education for
achieving his goal of black social improvement (Spivey 1978, 50–51). As
quoted in Franklin (1973, 285), Washington believed that black education
"should be so directed that the greatest proportion of the mental strength of
the masses will be brought to bear upon the everyday practical things of life,
upon something that is needed to be done, and something which *they will be
permitted to do* in the community in which they reside" (emphasis added).

The basic philosophy of industrial education as practiced at Hampton and
Tuskegee was quite simple. The training in various domestic and trade skills
within an authoritarian and religiously based environment would produce a
black who would fit into the lower end of the occupational structure and, more
important, know his or her place among whites and come to accept that place
as proper.

Such a form of education was just what white society sought. For Southerners, it would keep blacks subservient and exploitable. For Northerners, it
would serve as a way of calming racial tensions and providing a well-trained
laboring underclass that could be used in the effort to industrialize the South.
For these reasons, wealthy philanthropists in both the North and the South
were willing to give large grants to institutions that adopted this vocational
model while ignoring those institutions which remained academically oriented (Quarles 1969; Winston 1971; Franklin 1973).

The results were as dramatic as they were devastating. The ideology of vocational education became the panacea for the race problem in America. Except for a few institutions of higher learning (Fisk, Atlanta, and Howard),
black colleges took the financial windfalls and adopted the vocational curriculum. Educationally, vocational training was a failure: it not only failed to prepare blacks to move up in society, but it also guaranteed that they would move
down. The emphasis on manual training and the trades served to destroy the
educational aspirations that had been aroused during Reconstruction and

wiped out the hope that education could provide a way out of poverty. By 1930 industrial education was seen as a "cynical political strategy, not a sound educational policy" and proved to be the "great detour" for blacks from which they are just beginning to return (Winston 1971, 683).

Scientific Careers

The few blacks who managed to overcome educational obstacles and enter careers in science and technology still faced bigotry in other aspects of their lives. This discrimination extended to the lack of public recognition of names and accomplishments of black scientists, medical researchers, and inventors. Only recently have scholars begun to search out evidence of these blacks' contributions and discover that, although blacks are rare in the history of American science, they are by no means missing or negligible. It is worth noting that, for many of the same kinds of reasons, the presence and activities of women in science were long overlooked by historians and only recently have been reexamined (Rossiter 1974).

It is appropriate to describe briefly the work of some of these black American scientists and inventors and to examine the ways in which they surmounted the formidable barriers to intellectual achievement.

Before the Civil War, the United States was not known for its scientific accomplishments. It would not make sense to expect blacks to be the exception to this rule. For most slaves and free blacks, the main issue was gaining and keeping their freedom. Many blacks with exceptional abilities directed their talents to devising ways to gain their own freedom and to interest others in supporting such efforts. Inevitably, preachers and orators outnumbered inventors among the black community during the antebellum period (Baker 1917; Bardolph 1955).

But it is also true that black inventors, especially in the South, were unrecognized by historians. Slaves who invented mechanical devices to relieve the physical burden of labor could not protect their rights to the inventions (Baker 1917). They were not recognized as citizens and therefore could not enter into contracts. The federal government refused to grant them patents or to allow them to transfer patent rights to their owners. This did not preclude the outright theft of inventions by the slave owners, who would claim them as their own. Given this situation, it can never be known how many inventions were originated by slaves (Haber 1970). Among free blacks, inventors preferred to have their race kept secret for fear that the information would impair the commercial success of their devices (Baker 1913).

The government restriction on the granting of patents to slaves did not apply to free blacks. For example, James Forten (1766–1842), a free black Philadelphian, had no difficulty in getting a patent for his invention for handling sails or deriving a comfortable living from its manufacture. The same could be said of Norbert Rillieux. Born in New Orleans 17 March 1806, Rillieux was the son of Vincent Rillieux, a wealthy plantation owner, and his slave Constance Vivant. Because of his father's position, the young Rillieux had the advantages of both freedom and wealth. He attended Catholic schools in New Orleans and studied engineering in France. At the age of twenty-four he became the youngest instructor in applied mechanics at L'Ecole Centrale in Paris and contributed papers on steam technology to engineering journals (A. E. Klein 1971). His major accomplishment came in 1846 when he invented and patented a vacuum pan that transformed the process of refining sugar. The device yielded a superior product—granulated sugar—at a low price. The invention was a boon to the sugar industry in Louisiana and revolutionized the production of sugar worldwide (Baker 1917; Haber 1970; Toppin 1971; Ploski and Williams 1983).

A discussion of early black inventors cannot fail to mention the accomplishments of Benjamin Banneker. The son of a free black mother and a slave she had purchased, Banneker was born in Baltimore County, Maryland, in 1731. Taught to read and write at home by his grandmother, Banneker also attended an integrated public school where he obtained the equivalent of an eighth grade education. His curiosity about mechanical devices led him in 1761 to construct a wooden striking clock so accurately made that it kept perfect time for over twenty years. His knowledge of astronomy and his mathematical ability enabled him to predict the solar eclipse of 1789. And during the next ten years he published an almanac of tide tables, eclipses, and medicinal formulas. His most notable contribution came as a surveyor with the team chosen by George Washington to develop the plans for the new national capital. Although publicly recognized in France and England for his scientific accomplishments, he received little official recognition in the United States—although in 1970 Banneker Circle in Washington, D.C., was named in his honor (Haber 1970; Toppin 1971; Ploski and Williams 1983).

During the second half of the nineteenth century, a number of black inventors produced devices of considerable importance in the mechanical advance of American industry. Most noteworthy are Lewis Latimer, Granville T. Woods, Elijah McCoy, and Jan Earnst Matzeliger.

Jan Matzeliger, born in Dutch Guiana in 1852, emigrated to Philadelphia at the age of ten and went to work in a shoe factory. He realized that, while the tops and bottoms of shoes were being manufactured by machine, the two parts had to be put together by hand—a time-consuming bottleneck in the production process. He spent long hours at great physical and financial cost to do the seemingly impossible—invent a machine that would sew the top and bottom halves of manufactured shoes together. After Matzeliger developed his lasting machine, it was possible for one factory to produce 150 to 700 pairs of shoes a day, compared to 50 pairs sewn by hand. The cost of shoes went down, and the American shoe industry grew dramatically. Matzeliger died in 1889 at the age of 37 and never realized any of the millions of dollars that eventually derived from his invention (Kaplan 1955; Haber 1970; Logan and Winston 1982; Ploski and Williams 1983).

Elijah McCoy was born in Canada in 1844 to runaway slaves. He attended grammar schools in Michigan and went to Scotland to apprentice as a mechanical engineer. Upon returning to America, McCoy found that because of his race it was impossible for him to find employment as an engineer. He eventually took a job as fireman on the Michigan Central Railroad where his experiences with maintaining the locomotive engines inspired him to invent a device that solved a critical problem in the manufacturing industry. Heavy machinery constantly needs lubrication to prevent the metal parts from fusing together. In the late nineteenth century, factory workers would have to stop the machines and lubricate the parts by hand, a time-consuming and costly procedure. McCoy invented the "lubricating cup," which provided continuous and automatic lubrication of moving parts. His inventions were significant in perfecting the overall lubrication system eventually used in all large industrial plants with heavy machinery. Over a period of forty years McCoy acquired more than fifty patents for his lubrication devices, yet he died poor, as his race made it difficult for him to realize any profit from the inventions that made millions for others. Although not documented, it is often claimed that the expression "It's the real McCoy" is associated with his devices (Haber 1970; Ploski and Williams 1983).

In the area of electrical engineering, Granville T. Woods and Lewis Latimer deserve special recognition. Born in Ohio in 1856, Granville T. Woods attended school until the age of ten. First employed in a machine shop, he continued to develop his mechanical aptitude working on the railroad and reading books on electricity in his spare time. He reportedly took a course in electrical and mechanical engineering, but was essentially self-taught. He invented a telephone transmitter in 1884, but is best known for his development of the Synchronous Multiplex Railway Telegraph. This system enabled communication between stations and moving trains and greatly improved railway safety. In the twenty-year period from 1879 to 1899, twenty-three separate inventions bore his name, including the overhead conduction system for electric railways and the "third rail" used in most subway systems. Known as the "Black Edison," he held over sixty patents, many of which were assigned to General Electric, Westinghouse, and Bell Telephone (Haber 1970; Toppin 1971; Logan and Winston 1982; Ploski and Williams 1983).

Lewis Howard Latimer was born in Massachusetts in 1848. At the age of ten, Latimer was forced to quit school and help support his family. After serving in the United States Naval Service during the Civil War, he was employed as an office boy with Crosby & Gould, Patent Solicitors. Demonstrating his superior skill after reluctantly being given the chance to try his hand at drafting, Latimer ultimately was named chief draftsman. Needing a skilled draftsman to help prepare his patent application, Alexander Graham Bell asked Latimer to prepare the drawings and descriptions for the telephone patent issued in 1876. Latimer eventually began to work on his own inventions, and in 1881 he developed a method of making carbon filaments that were longer lasting than previous filaments, greatly improving Edison's incandescent lamps. He supervised the installation of electric lights in New York, Philadelphia, Montreal, and London. In 1884 Latimer joined the Edison Company, where he was instrumental in defending Edison's patents in court (Haber 1970; Logan and Winston 1982; Ploski and Williams 1983).

Most of the black scientists and inventors of the nineteenth century were very gifted, self-taught individuals who lacked academic or professional training in the physical sciences. This should not be surprising since the description would apply equally to white American scientists and inventors at the same time. In fact, it was only in 1861 that the first doctorate was granted in a science—physics—at Yale University. Probably the most noteworthy accomplishment in the history of blacks in science occurred just fifteen years later. In 1876 Edward Alexander Bouchet, a twenty-four-year-old black man, was awarded a Ph.D. in physics from Yale University for a dissertation in geometrical optics entitled *On Measuring Refracting Indices*. Bouchet was the first black to receive a doctorate from an American university and only the sixth person in the United States to be awarded a Ph.D. in physics. Yet, other than an occasional footnote in the history of black education, Bouchet and his accomplishments remain virtually unknown to the world of science and literally unheard of by the world in general. What happened to Bouchet provides a glimpse into the adversity facing educated blacks in post–Civil War America.

Edward Bouchet was born in 1852 to free parents in New Haven, Connecticut, where he attended a public "colored school." Like most of the schools for blacks in the city, it was small, ungraded, and had only one teacher. In 1868 Bouchet was the first black to be accepted into Hopkins Grammar School, a preparatory school for the classical and scientific departments at Yale College. During his two years at Hopkins he studied Latin and Greek grammar, geometry, algebra, and Greek history. He graduated in 1870 first in his class and was chosen valedictorian (Bechtel 1986).

Bouchet entered Yale in the fall of 1870 and continued to excel. When he graduated in 1874, his grade-point average was 3.22 on a 4.0-point scale, the sixth highest in a class of 124. In 1875 Bouchet returned to Yale to pursue graduate work in physics. During his two years in the graduate school, he paid special attention to chemistry, mineralogy, and experimental physics. Under the direction of Arthur Wright, he successfully completed his dissertation (Bechtel 1986).

Bouchet's graduate education was encouraged and financed by Alfred Cope, a member of the board of managers of a Friends school for blacks in Philadelphia, the Institute for Colored Youth (ICY). Firm believers in the value of liberal education and the unlimited capabilities of blacks, Cope and the other managers offered at ICY a curriculum that included ancient history, geography, Greek and Latin classics, algebra, geometry, and chemistry. In an effort to expand the school's offerings, Cope established a Scientific Fund to promote learning in the principles of applied science. It was the establishment of the Scientific Fund that led Cope to invite Bouchet to head the new science program (Perkins 1978).

Bouchet arrived in Philadelphia in the fall of 1876 and taught at the ICY for the next twenty-six years. However, as with all American blacks during the last two decades of the nineteenth century, Bouchet's life took a turn for the worse. By the mid-1890s, many Philadelphia Quakers were becoming disillusioned with the black community as they now questioned the ability of blacks to respond to the efforts being made on their behalf. In 1894 a study made of the institute's curriculum suggested that it be simplified, stating that the courses were "pitched too high." By the end of the century, the new managers had become openly hostile to classical and academic education and receptive to Booker T. Washington's educational philosophy. In their efforts to redirect the ICY along the line of industrial training at Hampton and Tuskegee, the managers proceeded to fire all the teachers, including Bouchet, and replaced them with instructors favorable to industrial education (Perkins 1978; Bechtel 1986).

No white college would have considered him seriously for a position on its faculty even with his superior qualifications. But barriers other than race had an impact on Bouchet's career. The ascendance of vocational-industrial instruction during the latter half of the nineteenth century, and the overwhelming acceptance of the Hampton-Tuskegee model for blacks in particular, served to limit Bouchet's opportunities. His academic education and his training in the natural sciences made him increasingly unattractive as a candidate at black colleges that had adopted the industrial-education philosophy. As noted by DuBois (1973, 65), the debate between academic and industrial education for blacks was a bitter one. "The disputants came to rival organizations, to severe social pressure, to anger and even to blows. . . . Employment and promotion depended often on a Negro's attitude toward industrial education. . . . Men were labeled and earmarked by the allegiance to one school of thought or to the other."

The difficulties that the industrial-education movement created for Bouchet were tragic not only for him but also for the generations of students he might have trained in science. The movement stopped students from striving for professional careers; it perpetuated stereotypes about black intellectual inferiority; and it kept blacks in economically inferior jobs. Even on its own terms, it misjudged the demand for blacks in the trades, arousing the hostility of white workers. It failed to see that the rise of the large corporation would put many tradesmen and craftsmen out of business (DuBois 1973; Franklin 1973).

Although whites enthusiastically endorsed industrial training for blacks and helped to implement it through contributions to black schools, it is noteworthy that some blacks resisted. W. E. B. DuBois led this movement against industrial education, while leaders at some black colleges refused to change their curriculum in the direction of Tuskegee and Hampton. An important change occurred at the beginning of the twentieth century as a small number of men and women began to move into the fields of science and engineering. Consider, for example, three blacks who made significant contributions to biology and medicine: E. E. Just, Percy Julian, and Charles Drew.

Born in Charleston, South Carolina, in 1883, Ernest Just received his bachelor's degree with honors from Dartmouth. In college he developed an interest in biology, especially cell structure and development. After graduating from Dartmouth, he taught biology at Howard University and began a twenty-year period of summer research at the Marine Biological Laboratories at Woods Hole, Massachusetts. In 1916 he received his Ph.D. in biology from the University of Chicago. During his career he published two books and over sixty papers in scholarly journals. His ideas on cell-membrane activity completely changed the scientific opinion of his time as he successfully demonstrated that the cell's cytoplasm and ectoplasm are equally important as the nucleus in heredity. As with most of the black scientists of the period, Just never received proper recognition in the United States, although he was respected and honored in the scientific capitals of Europe (Haber 1970; Toppin 1971; Ploski and Williams 1983; Manning 1983).

Born in Alabama in 1899, Percy Julian attended DePauw University, where he was valedictorian and Phi Beta Kappa. He taught at Fisk, Howard, and West Virginia State College before attending Harvard and the University of Vienna. A specialist in derivative and synthetic drugs, Julian discovered cortisone, a cheap and effective treatment for arthritis derived from soybean oil. In 1935 Julian was the first to synthesize physostigmine, important in the treatment of glaucoma. He was also the first to synthesize hormones, greatly reducing the cost of these drugs and making them available to thousands of people who were unable to afford the expensive natural drugs. He was offered the post of chief chemist and director of research for the Glidden Company in Chicago, the first black scientist to obtain such a prestigious position. This was a turning point in the struggle of black scientists to gain access to America's research facilities (Haber 1970; Toppin 1971; Ploski and Williams 1983).

Charles Drew, medical doctor and researcher, was educated at Amherst College in Massachusetts and took his medical degree from McGill University in Canada. Early in his career, he became interested in the problems associated with the transfusion and storage of blood. He took a teaching position at Howard University, and while working on his doctor of science degree at Columbia wrote a dissertation on banked blood. He soon became an expert on separating and storing blood, and his research on blood plasma is credited with saving many lives during World War II. In 1941 he was called to England to help with the problems of blood storage and set up the first blood bank in England. Drew was one of the first blacks to become a diplomate in surgery and the first black to be appointed an examiner by the American Board of Surgery (Haber 1970; Toppin 1971; Ploski and Williams 1983).

To this discussion of unrecognized scientists must be added several others. One is Charles H. Turner, who received his doctorate from the University of Chicago in 1907. He published many papers in the area of animal behavior, and the phenomenon of insect activity referred to as "Turner's circling" is named for him. William A. Hinton was an authority on venereal disease and responsible for developing the Hinton Test for detecting syphilis. In 1949 he became the first black professor of medicine at Harvard. Lloyd A. Hall was chief chemist and director of research for Griffith Laboratories in Chicago. He transformed the meatpacking industry with his development of curing salts for processing and preserving meats. Louis Tompkins Wright was a leading surgeon and medical researcher best known for his work in developing the intradermal method of smallpox vaccination. He also pioneered in drug therapy for cancer, and was the first to use chlortetracycline on humans. A graduate of Harvard Medical School, Wright was the first black to be appointed to the staff of New York Hospital and the second black to be elected to a fellowship in the American College of Surgeons (Haber 1970; Logan and Winston 1982; Ploski and Williams 1983).

There is little doubt that white scientists of this caliber won recognition from the scientific world in the form of research grants, prestigious positions and prizes. More important, they were urged to continue their research and their teaching of future scientists. In light of the racism and discrimination these black scientists faced, their accomplishments are even more impressive, yet their names and deeds remain obscure. Students quickly learn the importance of such men as Benjamin Franklin, Eli Whitney, Thomas Edison, Alexander Graham Bell, and Jonas Salk. These individuals are held up as great scientists and inventors whose work was instrumental in the transformation of American society. Students rarely learn the names Benjamin

Banneker, Norbert Rillieux, Granville T. Woods, Lewis Latimer, or Percy Julian, or their equally important contributions to the transformation of American science and industry.

The achievements of black intellectuals and scientists in white America have been largely hidden, ignored, or diminished in importance. The world of science and research was the private domain of white males. Society provided blacks with more appropriate arenas for gaining success and notoriety, arenas more fitting their place in the American social order. The roles of gladiator and jester have long been traditional among powerless people and are seen often by the dominant group as more appropriate than that of scholar or scientist (Lewis 1972). According to the stereotype, blacks were to perform, produce, or entertain, not invent, design, or create. The former activities require only simple innate abilities; the latter intelligence and creativity—characteristics not thought to be present in blacks.

From the perspective of white America at the turn of the century, educated and intellectual blacks presented a grave problem. They were not supposed to exist, and the fact that they did exist challenged the very foundation of the white belief in black intellectual and social inferiority (Winston 1971). Therefore, such individuals had to be explained away (they were called freaks), minimized (they were accused of stealing their ideas from whites), hidden (they were not acknowledged), or destroyed (they suffered discrimination and violence). The lives of the early black scientists were filled not only with the challenge and elation of scientific discovery, but with the specter of racism and discrimination as well.

During his brief tenure at St. Paul's College in Lawrenceville, Virgina, Edward Bouchet was respected and admired in the community. Nevertheless, he was assaulted by a white lawyer he accidentally bumped into as they came around a corner (Bechtel 1986). Percy Julian was denied appointment as head of DePauw's chemistry department because he was black, and he would not go to Appleton, Wisconsin, for a job interview because of a city statute prohibiting blacks from staying overnight. During his tenure at Glidden, his house in Oakbrook was set afire and bombed in several acts of racial violence. Ernest Just, despite his scientific discoveries, was never offered an appointment at a major American research center or university and was urged by whites to teach at Black universities in order to help his race (Haber 1970; Logan and Winston 1982; Manning 1983).

More important than these acts of racism toward individuals are the patterns of institutional discrimination that created an almost insurmountable obstacle to the black scientist. Segregation produced isolation: black Ph.D.s in science were forced to teach in black colleges and high schools, which were often unsympathetic to the needs of a research scientist. Edward Bouchet and Charles Turner spent most of their careers in high schools with limited resources and poorly equipped labs. Those who were fortunate enough to find positions in black colleges (like Just or Julian) often taught students from the inner city or rural areas, who lacked advanced training in mathematics and English. These teachers seldom had the scientist's pleasure of training students to surpass their mentors. The black colleges had little money available for scientific equipment or libraries. In the South, where most black colleges were located, black scholars were denied use of public libraries and white university laboratories and were barred from local chapters of learned societies (Julian 1969; Winston 1971).

To this can be added Jim Crow laws designed to restrict the social and political actions of blacks, the constant threat of violence reinforced by numerous lynchings every year, and the exclusion from the community of science in general. In this type of restricted and fearful environment, the Ph.D. degree was a farce (Julian 1969). Excluded because of their race from full participation in the American scientific community, these scientists languished in obscurity.

Under such historical conditions, it is no wonder that so few blacks chose to study science. Ernest Just's motives in discouraging his students from pursuing careers in science grew out of his own bitter recognition of the reality they faced (Winston 1971; Manning 1983). For blacks at the turn of the century, education had to provide marketable skills, a point of view that continues to direct scientifically talented students into careers in education, medicine, or law rather than biology, physics, or chemistry. For any black who knew about Just, Julian, or Turner, the lesson was clear: Even those with the highest level of education and degrees from America's most prestigious universities were denied the recognition and respect befitting their qualifications and scientific accomplishments. In the fields of medicine, teaching, and law, one could find jobs and prosper, albeit while restricted to serving a black clientele. Under the rules made by whites concerning the roles blacks were to play in American society, the pragmatic black decided it was better to be an employed teacher or lawyer than an underemployed scientist.

Specific evidence supports this argument. Edwards (1959), in a survey of three hundred black professionals, found that half of the respondents had given serious consideration to careers other than the one they presently had. Many expressed a primary interest in becoming engineers, architects, or research scientists, but felt that blacks could not earn a decent living in these occupations. One of Edwards's respondents, a physicist now working as a teacher, had wanted to enter the field of engineering. He changed his mind when it became clear that despite his ranking near the top of the class, white classmates who were far below him could get jobs as student laboratory technicians while he could not.

The black scientist is both rare and relatively unknown: rare because of an educational philosophy that produced laborers not scholars, and unknown because white society has often refused to recognize the contributions of those able to overcome the obstacles placed before them. In part, this failure to recognize the black scientist stems from beliefs about black inferiority. To acknowledge these individuals would be to demonstrate the fallacy of those beliefs and the error of the policies that deprived blacks of equal and quality education.

Separate, unequal, and discriminatory educational policies served to keep a generation of blacks at the bottom socially, politically, and economically. And while a few (such as Bouchet, Just, and Julian) were able to break through and acquire a quality education, being black meant that in most instances the rewards were withheld. The rare black scientist was faced with a lack of research facilities, funds, and recognition for achievements that by any standard were of superior quality and importance. Given the historical conditions, one can understand why black scientists were treated in such a manner. But to understand is not to justify. Educational policies served to suppress and demoralize generations of blacks in America, creating discredible castes within an ostensibly open society.

History is more than description and explanation; one can often use the past to examine the present. What has the past taught with regard to current educational policies directed toward blacks? Several major themes can be identified. First are *interest* and *motivation*. Historical evidence shows that blacks in America had a strong interest in and motivation for getting an education. This desire continues as large numbers of blacks seek higher education. Second is *opportunity*. The evidence is just as clear that blacks were denied the opportunity for a quality education by legal and extralegal means. Today, blacks are able to take advantage of educational opportunities as many of the barriers of the past have been removed. And third, is the *reward* or *payoff*. Given the historical conditions, for most blacks there was no payoff for getting an education. Today, the picture appears more positive as blacks are found in all professions and at all levels of achievement.

Yet, below the surface a different image can be seen. Less than 2 percent of all doctoral scientists in America are black, and few black students take courses in the sciences or express a desire to pursue such careers. For those who complete graduate school, the door to a science career is opened. The problem, as in the past, remains at the level of basic educational opportunity and experience. America has desegregated its white schools and has renounced its past practices as counterproductive and mean-spirited. But those practices remain, in effect, in the form of tracking, curriculum reform, and teacher expectations.

Eighty years ago, vocational education served to perpetuate black social and economic inferiority, locking a generation of blacks into low-paying, low-status jobs. Today black children are bused to excellent schools in an attempt to equalize educational opportunity. Yet once off the bus and in the school, they are tracked, counseled, or intimidated away from academic courses into less rigorous curricula. At the turn of the century, the typical student at Hampton or Tuskegee learned simple trades and domestic skills, while outside American industry was going through a transformation that was making those skills obsolete. Today, the typical black student studies a watered-down curriculum devoid of higher-level math and science courses, while outside the computer is transforming the world into a more complex and scientifically sophisticated arena.

To break the hold of the past, parents, educators, and policymakers need to move forward and address the educational deficiencies that continue to derail the science careers of black students in America. This book provides a look at the current situation of science and math education and opportunity as it pertains to blacks. Using the most recent data, the authors demonstrate that blacks remain outside of science, math, and engineering careers; discuss the reasons for this continued underrepresentation; and provide suggestions for improving minority representation in the sciences.

STUDENT PARTICIPATION

JOSEPHINE D. DAVIS

1

The Mathematics Education
of Black High School Students

The status of mathematics education for black students is of major concern to educators, researchers, and policymakers. Blacks are more likely than whites to drop out of the educational pipeline at every major transition point (Berryman 1985). Those who remain in school study fewer advanced mathematics courses and are more likely to repeat the courses that they do study. Black students score the lowest of all racial groups on standardized tests of achievement in mathematics. Yet recent research findings and some federal initiatives show that blacks can achieve at levels comparable to others when given equality of opportunity to learn mathematics (Malcom 1984).

The problem of low mathematics achievement among blacks, although most often explained by course enrollment trends (National Assessment of Educational Progress 1983; Jones, Burton, and Davenport 1984), derives from a complex of interdependent factors. Course enrollment decisions are affected by such student- and parent-related factors as family educational background and socioeconomic status, cognitive learning style, career aspirations, and self-concept in mathematics. Students whose parents have medium to high income levels or have attended college, for example, are more likely than those at lower levels to study mathematics beyond Algebra I and Geometry.

On the other hand, such school-related factors as classroom environment, resources, organization, racial composition, and quality of the curriculum and school personnel lessen the effects of these student- and parent-related factors.

The author gratefully acknowledges the valuable assistance of Rebecca Zwick, research scientist, and Judy Pollack, senior research data analyst, at the Educational Testing Service, Princeton, New Jersey. Special appreciation is also given to family members, Gordon, Josette, Monique, and Rodney for their support and encouragement.

It appears that blacks are initially interested in mathematics; however, long-term experiences with institutional barriers create psychological barriers that later lead to mathematics avoidance or exclusion.

Research shows that blacks have positive attitudes toward mathematics in the early grades (Beane 1985). These attitudes remain positive throughout the high school years but are not substantiated by course enrollment decisions at that level. Beginning in junior high school and becoming more pronounced during high school, mathematics avoidance or exclusion emerges as a serious problem, resulting in lower proficiency levels.

Overall, the evidence suggests that low mathematics achievement among blacks reflects the historical fact that most poor, disadvantaged, inner-city, low ability, or racial minority youth in America are not enrolled in schools that emphasize academic subjects. Many black students simply do not have the opportunity to learn mathematics or to experience across grade levels the sustained and systematic teaching of mathematics in intellectually challenging ways, as the following characterization by Carol Ascher (1983, 1) suggests:

> Whatever the term used for these disadvantaged students, and whatever the complex sources of their problems in mathematics, these low-income, inner city minorities or low achievers tend to be placed together early in their schooling and to be taught by the same instructional methods, by the same teachers, in the same classes, and their problems in mathematics rapidly become similar both diagnostically and in their treatment.

In short, mathematics achievement in America has not fulfilled the promise of curricular reform, regardless of the student's race. While white students' mathematics achievement, in the more than three decades since *Sputnik* was launched, has remained virtually unchanged, black students have made modest gains. Even so, blacks have continued to perform at much lower levels than any other racial group.

This lagging achievement needs to be understood. More research is needed—especially nationally sponsored, systematic research—which examines more clearly the relationship between mathematics achievement and the opportunity black students have to learn quality mathematics. Specifically, the historical and psychological barriers to the mathematics achievement of black students need to be identified and addressed by policy and practice, otherwise the mathematics achievement scores of black students will not improve significantly. The consistent failure of the nation to recognize and address this need is in itself a matter that warrants concern.

As a response to this need, data are presented on the mathematics achievement of black high school students relative to their mathematical training. They highlight variables associated with the opportunity to learn mathematics and show how these variables affect mathematics achievement. The data source is the third National Assessment of Educational Progress (NAEP). Results are based on the author's research study, *The Effect of Mathematics Course Enrollment on Racial/Ethnic Differences in Secondary School Mathematics* (Davis 1986). Following a brief historical overview of the mathematics reform movement, key variables are identified. A discussion of the study's methodology, findings, and recommendations are then presented. The status of computer education for blacks and an achievement model for seventeen-year-old black high school students of mathematics complete the chapter's presentation.

Historical Perspectives

Mathematics education in America has been in a dynamic state for more than three decades. Spurred by the launching of *Sputnik,* school mathematics was revolutionized in the 1960s. Introducing new content and innovative instructional strategies for teaching traditional mathematics, this new math initially provided hope for improved proficiency. At best, it only revitalized the mathematics classroom. Before the decade had ended, Scholastic Aptitude Test (SAT) scores revealed that basic mathematics competency had declined further than before the reform was implemented. Allendoerfer (1965) attributed this decline to the exclusive focus on the college-capable student. Ignoring theories of learning and educational research, this first revolution, Allendoerfer asserts, did not produce substantive changes.

The need for more remedial courses at the college level and the publication of *Why Johnny Can't Add* (Kline 1973) further documented widespread computational deficiencies. As a corrective measure, rote learning and drill-and-practice techniques were emphasized. During the 1970s, back-to-basics became fashionable. Teachers began to individualize instruction and to use behavioral objectives as attention turned increasingly to the less able learner. By the end of the decade, the number of blacks enrolled in remedial or developmental mathematics had increased sharply.

By the early 1980s, the National Council of Teachers of Mathematics recognized the need for professional educators to be more directly involved in establishing educational goals. Using research findings and a survey of the opinions of "many sectors of society," the National Council of Teachers of Mathematics (1980) established an agenda for school mathematics in the 1980s. The recommendations called for a focus on problem solving and a

TABLE 1.1   SAT-Mathematics Scores for College-Bound Seniors

Race/Ethnicity	1976	1977	1978	1979	1980	1981	1982
Black	354	357	354	358	360	362	366
White	493	489	483	483	482	483	483
Asian	518	514	510	511	509	513	513
Native American	420	421	419	421	426	425	424
Mexican-American	410	408	402	410	413	415	416
Puerto Rican	401	397	388	388	394	398	403
Other	458	457	450	447	449	447	449
Total	472	470	468	467	466	466	467

SOURCE: Biemiller 1982.
NOTE: Scores range from 200 to 800.

broadening of the conceptual development of basic skills beyond computational facility. The "New Basics" required proficiency in the analysis and interpretation of data, and skills in calculator and computer use.

Toward the middle of the 1980s, corporate managers, military commanders, and other employers became concerned that recent high school graduates were deficient in higher-order thinking and critical-reasoning skills. This "rising tide of mediocrity" was stressed by the National Commission on Excellence in Education in its report, *A Nation at Risk* (1983).

The report cited national achievement data similar to those presented in Table 1.1 to document declining achievement. Achievement declines on the SAT scores over a six-year period (1976 to 1982) were noted only for the traditional high achievers in mathematics—whites and Asians. Although trailing in achievement, racial and ethnic minorities demonstrated gains during the same period.

As determined from the data in Table 1.1, blacks, Native Americans, Mexican Americans, and Puerto Ricans achieved net gains of twelve, four, six, and two points, respectively, on the SAT-math over the six-year period. In part, these gains validate the gains made by federally funded intervention projects targeted at racial minorities. On the other hand, the SAT-math declines between 1976 and 1982 of ten points (from 493 to 483) for whites and five points (from 518 to 513) for Asians suggest the possibility of a general decline in the quality of mathematics training provided all American youth.

Despite these declines, the mean SAT-math score for whites in 1982 was 117 points above that attained by blacks (483 versus 366). While the general decline in the quality of mathematics training partly explains this achievement gap, the increased emphasis on remedial training for blacks during the late 1970s is a significant factor contributing to their trailing performance on the

SAT-math. Many blacks simply were not taught or exposed to much of the kind of material tested on the SAT-math.

NAEP (1983) documented similar results, relating differences in black/white achievement to patterns of course enrollment. Between NAEP's second and third national assessments of mathematics, the performance of black students increased by one percent (from 44 to 45 percent); white students' performance remained stable at 63 percent. Over the same period, the black/white achievement gap narrowed only one percentage point.

The actual achievement profile (Table 1.2) shows that gains for seventeen-year-old black high school students were made on the lower cognitive items measuring rote memory and quick recall. The group's highest proficiency level (63 percent) was attained at the knowledge level; black students who were enrolled in the most advanced courses attained the highest performance rating (75 percent). Overall, blacks demonstrated the greatest deficiencies at the applications level, where their achievement ranged from 21 to 39 percent. These data show that the study of advanced mathematics courses improves proficiency across each level of the cognitive domain.

Black youth continue to be challenged, however, by general problem-solving tasks based on real-world situations, measurement concepts, and geometry. Data representation, analysis, and interpretation also present difficulties in the classroom.

Meanwhile, history is repeated. Public demand for improved mathematics proficiency—this time stimulated by *A Nation at Risk*—has intensified mathematics reform. This report underscores the importance of a quality high school mathematics curriculum in developing latent talent to meet America's needs. Other national commissions and task forces, recognizing the need, joined the education commission. They also recommended increasing the number of mathematics courses required for high school graduation and the time devoted to studying a more rigorous and efficient mathematics curriculum (National Consortium for Educational Excellence 1984; National Science

TABLE 1.2   Math Performance Levels

Level	Total	Below Algebra I	Algebra I	Geometry	Algebra II	Above Algebra II
Knowledge	62.6%	56.6%	61.4%	66.6%	71.2%	75.3%
Skills	44.2	36.6	43.4	47.7	55.0	59.1
Understanding	44.8	35.6	43.9	49.6	55.5	61.4
Applications	26.0	20.9	24.9	27.7	31.2	38.8

SOURCE: NAEP 1983.
NOTE: Of seventeen-year-old blacks.

Board Commission on Precollege Education in Mathematics, Science, and Technology 1982a). Yet, of all the recommendations made by these national groups, not one focused on equity concerns.

Like other students, more blacks will be required to study the more advanced mathematics courses that are academically rigorous. Yet, unlike other students, blacks will have no assurances that (*a*) supportive structures will be available to preclude en masse failure; (*b*) revisions will be made in the content of advanced courses to compensate for skill deficiencies or that topics will be introduced as required to bridge knowledge gaps; (*c*) that the qualifications and expectations of teachers will be elevated to ensure meaningful learning experiences. As the College Entrance Examination Board (1985, vii) observed, "Although many of the legal barriers to educational opportunity have been removed, education—to a large extent—remains separate and unequal in the United States."

A mathematics educator, Usiskin (1985), recognized the need for courses to be revised to accommodate the needs of many minority students. He called for the teaching of more real-world problems and admonished that the dual challenges of meeting national recommendations for increased coursework and improved mathematics proficiency would require yet another revolution in school mathematics.

This time, however, the revolution should focus on the concerns of the black learner. It should be molded by results of enlightened research. Educators and policymakers should, in turn, utilize these data as tools for decision making, providing those concerned with assurance that the identified needs of black learners will be met. To this end, some key variables that can be addressed by policy in the mathematics education of black high school students are identified.

Variables of Interest

Many educators agree that academic tracking prepares students for different careers. While it is generally known that students enrolled in the academic curriculum study more mathematics than those in other tracks (College Entrance Examination Board 1985; National Science Foundation 1984), it is now also known that the quality of advanced mathematics coursework in the academic curriculum is more competitive than advanced training in the general or vocational curriculum. Students in the academic curriculum achieve at higher levels than others. Rock et al. (1984) found that mathematics declines from 1972 to 1980 were related to enrolling in schools that deemphasized academics, not enrolling in college preparatory courses, and enrolling in the vocational or general curriculum.

The fact that enrollment in advanced mathematics courses improves mathematics achievement for all students has been well documented (Carpenter et al. 1980; Davis 1986; Jones, Burton, and Davenport 1984; Matthews et al. 1984). The more students persist in higher mathematics, the greater their achievement scores. Kulm (1980) also found that mathematics achievement is enhanced by mathematics self-concept. The perception of one's ability to do mathematics and the perception of oneself as a mathematics student are components of self-concept that may be influenced by classroom processes. Policy can address variances in classroom processes, academic tracking, and course enrollment practices. These variables will be used to determine the opportunities that black seventeen-year-old respondents to NAEP's *Third National Mathematics Assessment* (1983) had to learn mathematics. Their achievement will be examined from this perspective using results of the Davis (1986) study.

Methodology

The nationally representative sample for the study consisted of 14,289 seventeen-year-old high school students, of whom 76 percent were white, 16 percent were black, and 6 percent were Hispanic. The remaining 2 percent were "other races." Fifty-one percent of the sample were male. Student data included such demographic information as age, gender, ethnicity, parental educational level, and educational resources in the home. School data included the size and type of community, type of school, and region of the country. Achievement data were derived from respondents' correct responses to NAEP mathematics items, which were categorized into pre-algebra and algebra subtests. Written in open-ended or multiple-choice format, these items covered material normally learned in the eighth, ninth, and tenth grades.

Based on self-reported data of mathematics courses that were studied for at least one-half year, a mathematics course classification schema from advanced (A to D) to lower-level mathematics courses (E to H) was determined. Mathematics course enrollment constituted the primary independent variable, and the dependent variable was the mean percentage of correct responses to the pre-algebra and algebra subtests.

Findings

Table 1.3 shows student enrollment by type of curriculum and race. Black students were more likely to be enrolled in the general curriculum (47 percent); on the contrary, whites were more likely to be enrolled in the academic

TABLE 1.3   Academic Tracking

Race	Academic		General		Vocational	
	N	%	N	%	N	%
Black	790	36	1,013	47	2,173	18
White	4,884	46	4,355	43	1,192	11

NOTE: Of seventeen-year-olds by race.

TABLE 1.4   Secondary Mathematics Course Enrollment

	Academic		General		Vocational	
	N	Wtd.%	N	Wtd.%	N	Wtd.%
Black:						
Advanced	254	55%	123	16%	45	18%
Low	201	45%	617	84%	199	82%
Total	455	100%	740	100%	244	100%
White:						
Advanced	2,021	79%	1,032	31%	212	24%
Low	474	21%	2,114	69%	625	76%
Total	2,495	100%	3,146	100%	837	100%

NOTE: Levels by curriculum and race.

curriculum (46 percent). Significant racial differences favored white over black enrollment in the academic curriculum, whereas enrollment differences in the vocational curriculum favored blacks.

Student enrollment in advanced and lower-level mathematics courses is given by type of curriculum in Table 1.4. Although most students in the general and vocational curricula tended to enroll in low rather than advanced courses, proportionately more blacks than whites were enrolled in lower-level mathematics courses. For example, compared to 69 percent of whites in the general curriculum, 84 percent of the blacks enrolled in lower-level mathematics courses. The data confirm previous findings that proportionately more students in the academic curriculum take advanced mathematics. However, for blacks, only 10 percent more students (55 percent versus 45 percent) were so enrolled compared to 58 percent of the whites (79 percent versus 21 percent).

A more in-depth view of students' enrollment patterns within the academic curriculum is provided in Figure 1.1. Vertical bar graphs indicate the proportion of students enrolled in a particular mathematics course sequence by race;

horizontal lines show the overall racial distribution within the academic curriculum. Of the students in the academic curriculum who were enrolled in the most advanced mathematics course sequence, Sequence A—consisting of Algebra I, Algebra II, Geometry, and Trigonometry—89 percent were white, 9 percent were black, and 2 percent were Hispanic. Blacks were generally underrepresented in the remaining sequences (through Sequence D) of courses above the level of Algebra I. Most striking, however, is the finding that 34 percent of those seventeen-year-olds who had not studied any high school mathematics by their junior year were blacks. The range of the ratio of white to black enrollment across these course sequences ranged from 10:1 in Sequence A to 2:1 in Sequence E—those students who studied only Algebra I and General Business. A 2:1 ratio was also determined in Sequence F—those students who studied only Algebra I.

This determination of student enrollment by course sequences also demonstrated unexpected gaps in mathematical training. When prerequisite courses were not controlled, a less refined partitioning of the NAEP sample revealed that most blacks (43 percent) discontinued the study of mathematics after Algebra I. Among whites, 50 percent continued studying mathematics beyond Algebra II.

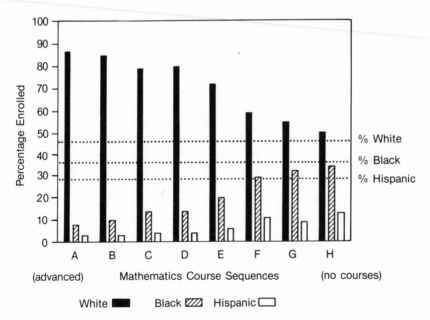

FIGURE 1.1   Mathematics Course Enrollment Pattern (by Race/Ethnicity)

College-bound students studying advanced mathematics courses benefit from academically challenging classrooms, higher levels of teacher expectation, and more enrichment experiences. Less potent experiences are provided in advanced mathematics courses offered in the vocational or general curriculum. Lower-level courses tend to emphasize the development of computational facility. Because most blacks in this sample studied low mathematics courses in the vocational and general curriculum, they did not encounter academically challenging mathematical experiences.

These data show a double-tiered barrier to opportunity for black high school students to study mathematics at the level required for improved mathematics proficiency on standardized examinations. First, disproportionately fewer blacks were enrolled in the academic curriculum. Second, even when enrolled in the academic curriculum, disproportionately more blacks compared to whites were in low-level mathematics courses.

Mathematics Achievement

Increasing trends in achievement were confirmed, as shown in Figure 1.2. The more advanced the mathematics courses, the higher the level of proficiency demonstrated by students on the assessment. However, compared to a 33 percent range for white students across Sequences A through H, a 27 percent range was found for blacks. Moreover, disparities in outcomes were found at each course sequence level. It is observed that white students in Sequence H (those who studied no mathematics) achieved at a level competitive with black students who had studied two courses—Sequence E (General Business and Algebra I). Thus, merely enrolling in the same courses (by titles) provides no assurance that achievement scores will equalize.

Table 1.5 provides data on racial differences in performance on the overall NAEP mathematics assessment by level of course sequence in which the student was enrolled. Significant size effects of the mean differences were found. The greatest difference was found in the achievement of students who studied only General Business (Sequence G). Significant achievement difference at the level of Sequence A is attributable primarily to pre-algebra deficiencies exhibited by blacks. Observe, too, that this difference is more than twice that found for students who studied no mathematics at the high school level (Sequence H).

The fact that racial differences increased as the course difficulty increased suggests that the schooling process is not equitably addressing students learning needs. The data show that persistence in mathematics improves achievement, regardless of race. Nonetheless, for blacks, accumulated deficiencies

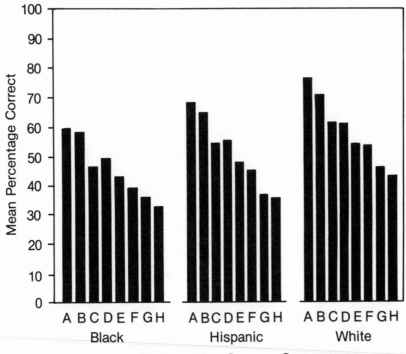

FIGURE 1.2   Performance on Total Test (by Race/Ethnicity)

preclude their closing the achievement gap. The content of advanced mathematics must be revised to address this need.

In Table 1.6, student achievements on the pre-algebra and algebra tests are given by racial composition of the school. Students attending predominantly white high schools attained significantly higher pre-algebra and total test scores than those attending predominantly black high schools. A moderate but significant difference was found on the pre-algebra test for whites attending predominantly white schools compared to whites attending predominantly black schools. Likewise, blacks attending predominantly white schools scored a significant 4 percent above blacks attending predominantly black schools (see Table 1.6).

Controlling for course enrollment, it was determined that achievement gains still favored blacks and whites who attended predominantly white high schools. The mean differences on the pre-algebra and total tests were significant for blacks enrolled in the most advanced courses (.62 and .67, respectively),

TABLE 1.5   Mathematics Achievement

Achievement differences disregarding courses enrolled				
	% difference[a]	Pooled s.d.	Mean s.e.	Effect size
White/black	18.7	16.6	0.5	1.10

White/black achievement differences by courses enrolled				
Course sequence	% difference[a]	Pooled s.d.	Mean s.e.	Effect size
A	17.2	11.2	2.2	1.5
B	12.7	11.9	1.4	1.1
C	15.3	15.0	2.1	1.0
D	12.1	12.2	1.7	1.0
E	11.4	12.8	1.1	0.9
F	14.9	12.3	1.3	1.2
G	10.7	6.9	0.6	1.6
H	10.6	18.1	2.6	0.6

NOTES: Racial/ethnic differences on the total test.
s.d. = standard deviation.
s.e. = standard error.
[a]Significant for = .01.

while similar effects occurred for white students enrolled in lower-level courses (.46 and .50, respectively). For whites, negligible achievement differences were found at the most advanced levels.

Whether due to the quality of instructional resources, availability of courses, talent of teachers, socioeconomic conditions, or parental influences, students attending predominantly white high schools received better training in pre-algebra skills than those who attended predominantly black high schools. In essence, advanced mathematics courses in predominantly white schools appear to better improve black students' pre-algebra skills than comparable courses in predominantly black schools. However, few blacks attending predominantly white schools were enrolled in advanced mathematics courses.

Prior course experiences or classroom processes may contribute to this problem of mathematics avoidance. The next section examines the nature of the mathematics classroom from the students' perspective. Their attitudes toward mathematics are examined in an effort to acquire insight into their self-concept in mathematics.

TABLE 1.6   Within-Group Comparisons of Mathematics Achievement

	Blacks				Whites			
Test	PW/PB diff. wtd. %	Pooled s.d.	Mean s.e.	Effect size	PW/PB diff. wtd. %	Pooled s.d.	Mean s.e.	Effect size
	Differences in mathematics achievement disregarding courses enrolled							
Pre-algebra	5.0[a]	17.1	.39	.29	6.4[a]	17.1	1.5	.37
Algebra	2.1	16.2	1.00	.13	4.4	20.4	1.8	.22
Total test	4.4[a]	15.3	.97	.29	6.1[a]	16.8	1.5	.36
	Difference in mathematics achievement course enrollment controlled							
Pre-algebra:								
A–D	8.6[a]	13.8	1.9	.62	1.5	12.7	2.2	.12
E–H	7.2[a]	14.5	1.4	.50	7.5[a]	16.4	2.3	.46
Algebra:								
A–D	6.0[a]	14.6	2.1	.41	3.0	15.3	2.7	.20
E–H	2.2	12.4	1.2	.18	4.4	15.1	2.1	.29
Total test:								
A–D	8.1[a]	12.1	1.7	.67	2.0	11.8	2.0	.17
E–H	6.1[a]	11.8	1.2	.52	7.2[a]	14.4	2.4	.50

NOTES: By racial composition of the school.   PW = predominantly white.
   s.d. = standard deviation.   PB = predominantly black.
   s.e. = standard error.
[a]Significant for = .01.

TABLE 1.7   Report of Classroom Experiences

	Predominantly black schools				Predominantly white schools			
	Course level A–D		Course level E–H		Course level A–D		Course level E–H	
	Black	*White*	*Black*	*White*	*Black*	*White*	*Black*	*White*
Teacher lecture	90%	78%	89%	85%	92%	79%	77%	67%
Textbook use	87	85	80	80	91	94	77	82
Homework done	60	49	41	47	72	73	54	54
Play games	10	0	5	5	3	4	1	1
Take tests	79	75	64	74	86	75	62	59
Wtd. *N*	45,907	19,527	103,680	22,473	44,762	678,244	125,466	742,719

NOTE: By race, school type, and course level—percent responding to the category "Often."

Mathematics Self-Concept

The data on affective items were obtained using the NAEP instrument. The weighted sample consisted of 149,587 blacks and 42,000 whites in predominantly black high schools and 170,228 blacks and 1,420,963 whites attending predominantly white high schools.

Instruction in mathematics classrooms consists of a daily routine of lecturing, board work, and textbook use, according to 80 percent of the students surveyed. Fewer than 10 percent of the students agreed that games were played often in their classes, even though most educators promote teaching mathematical games as an effective motivational technique for enhancing pre-algebra skills. In general, small to moderate differences were found in the reports of instructional experiences by race, school type, and level of courses, as shown in Table 1.7.

Students in advanced mathematics classes—regardless of race—used the textbook more often than those in low-level courses. At predominantly black schools, 87 percent of the blacks and 85 percent of the whites reported using the textbook "often," compared to 91 percent of the blacks and 94 percent of the whites who attended predominantly white schools. Slightly more of the advanced students at predominantly white schools reported using the textbook more often than their counterparts at predominantly black schools. Fewer blacks than whites enrolled in low-level courses at predominantly white schools used the textbook often.

Table 1.7 also shows a substantial difference in the reports of homework by race and by school composition. In predominantly white schools, 72 percent of the whites and 73 percent of the blacks did homework "often," compared to 60 percent of the blacks and 49 percent of the whites in predominantly black schools. The same pattern was observed for low-level students.

In this regard, the Davis (1986) study showed further that black students said that they were more willing than whites to work hard in mathematics (90 percent versus 79 percent). More blacks than whites felt that their parents wanted them to do well in mathematics (92 percent versus 86 percent). And black students were more likely to indicate "feeling good when solving a problem" (96 percent versus 89 percent). Moreover, 96 percent of the black students compared to 84 percent of the whites wanted to "do well" in mathematics. But only 58 percent of the blacks (54 percent of the whites) enjoyed mathematics. A sight majority of all students felt they were "good at mathematics," with 56 percent of the blacks and 58 percent of the whites agreeing to this statement. Of all the affective items listed, "being good at mathematics" was most highly correlated with achievement.

Black students have positive attitudes toward the study of mathematics—they have high expectations for themselves, as do their parents on their behalf.

They are willing to work hard in mathematics. Because only a slight majority "enjoys mathematics," or feels "good at mathematics," the mathematics self-concept among black students is not a strong one. Obviously the classroom experience is not encouraging or interesting enough (given the routine of lecturing, testing, board work, and no-games approach) to sustain the positive feeling these students are bringing to the classroom.

A Model of Mathematics Achievement

The model in Figure 1.3 considers mathematics achievement as a function of race or ethnicity, sex, socioeconomic status, and school processes. The last is prescribed in terms of enrollment by academic track, by mathematics courses, and by student effort as reflected by the amount of homework completed.

Validated by replications on three distinct sets of respondents, consisting of subsamples of more than 2,000 students each who responded to NAEP Mathematics Booklets 7, 11, and 13, the achievement model suggests that students can increase their mathematics proficiency through enrollment in advanced courses.

The magnitude and direction of the path coefficients in the model suggest that the relationship between background factors and achievement is due solely to the white male advantage. This relationship is explained by the historical interest this nation has had in high achievers in mathematics, traditionally the white male. Also, high socioeconomic status factors (parents' educational levels and educational materials in the home) favor enrollment in the academic curriculum and subsequently in advanced mathematics courses. Parents also tend to have higher achievement expectations for their sons than their daughters in mathematics (Rock et al. 1984).

An analysis of direct and indirect effects on mathematics achievement indicates that course enrollment has the greatest direct effect on achievement; however, the total effect of enrollment in the academic curriculum influenced by course experiences and homework results in the academic curriculum's being the best predictor of mathematics achievement. The direct effect of the parents' educational levels and the number of educational materials in the home (general socioeconomic status indicators) is marginally strengthened by school processes.

Earlier, NAEP data were used to show that blacks are learning more mathematics, but that the black/white achievement gap is not narrowing appreciably. Comprehensively viewed, the mathematics achievement and enrollment data presented point to a persistent and critical barrier to improved mathematics proficiency for blacks—the lack of opportunity to study mathematics

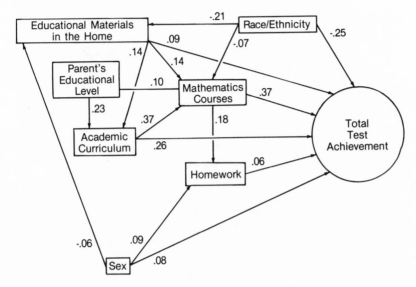

FIGURE 1.3   The Davis Achievement Model

courses that develop higher cognitive processes while adjusting for deficiencies in pre-algebra skills.

In view of the pervasive pre-algebra deficiencies among blacks, teachers and curriculum reformers are challenged to find innovative techniques for integrating real-world applications, data analysis, and higher-order thinking skills into the mathematics experiences of all black high school students. These experiences should be taught independent of the curriculum in which the student is enrolled. The advent of the computer in the classroom held the promise of improving mathematics learning, but studies now show that racial inequities are being reflected in computer training in ways identical to the secondary mathematics training of blacks.

Computer Training

Lockheed (1985), using the 1984 NAEP Computer Survey data base, found "few consistent" racial differences in computer course enrollment, frequency of computer use, or programming activities among seventeen-year-old high school students. She also determined that enrolling in a computer course and having a computer in the home were the only factors affecting computer use at school for seventeen-year-old eleventh graders.

Lockheed's results differ from Becker's findings (1983), which show that white students, particularly males, have the greatest access to computers. Becker also found that white males were more likely to have teacher-granted control to decide who uses the computer at school. Inequitable computer access has been documented in low-income schools (Anderson, Welch, and Harris 1984).

Black students are less likely to use computers for programming and more likely to use them for drill and practice. Baratz et al. (1985) found that predominantly black schools are less likely to use computers in instructional programs, to have computers available for student use, to offer computer courses, or to have computer-literate teachers.

In short, the variables found to influence mathematics achievement have also emerged as variables affecting computer literacy. School processes, course content, availability of courses, qualified teachers, and access to the opportunity to learn—owing to socioeconomic status factors and racial composition of the school—are again the variables of interest. Left uncorrected, this emerging gap in computer training and literacy will lead to even more limited career options for blacks in a society increasingly oriented toward technology.

The challenge of improving the mathematics and computer skills of black high school students can be met. Past and present federal initiatives, which provide challenging and interesting mathematics experiences for minorities, have improved performance. Blacks compete favorably with majority youth on standardized tests when provided the opportunity to study mathematics in meaningful ways.

Model Programs

In response to civil rights legislation of the 1960s, several federally sponsored projects and initiatives have been developed to improve black students' mathematics achievement. The National Science Foundation (NSF) has been a leading agency in this effort. NSF projects have been housed primarily on university or college campuses. Malcom et al. (1984) identified twenty-one such projects, 50 percent of which are devoted to high school instruction; 76 percent provide mathematics instruction. The goal of each project is to increase black representation in quantitative-based careers.

These projects feature action-oriented experiences. Mathematics is taught from an interdisciplinary perspective using hands-on activities as often as possible. Students talk mathematics and are very rarely engaged in drill and practice activities. Teachers and counselors are trained to integrate career awareness programs, emphasizing the relevance of mathematics, into regular classroom activities. Teachers also learn various strategies for teaching particular mathematical concepts. These training activities work together to improve student achievement.

One such exemplary project is the Mathematics Engineering Science Achievement project (MESA). Ninety percent of MESA graduates enrolled in college; of this number 66 percent pursued a math-based field. No significant differences in MESA and the statewide or national college-bound population were found. Follow-up activities show that the majority of MESA students in postsecondary institutions are in good academic standing and progressing normally.

In summary, mathematics reform in America has increased in intensity for more than three decades, but mathematics achievement has not fulfilled the promise of reform for any racial group, particularly blacks. Throughout their formative years, messages of being poor in mathematics combine with other forces to preclude black students' access to advanced mathematics courses by the time they reach high school.

The failure of black students to close the achievement gap with other students and the fact that blacks continue to achieve at levels below every other racial group after more than thirty years of mathematics reform in this country are reasons for concern. Now that the new technology—microcomputers—is falling short of expectations to improve blacks' mathematics skills and computer-literacy levels, there is even greater cause for alarm. The computer in the classroom reflects existing racial inequities in dramatically new ways. Because these inequities, left unaddressed, will result in further disenfranchisement of blacks from an increasingly technical society, all Americans should be concerned over the status of secondary mathematics and computer training of blacks.

For black youth, low mathematics achievement and now computer illiteracy are most directly related to factors that can be addressed by policies involving academic tracking, course enrollment practices, and school and classroom processes that mold mathematics self-concept.

Lessons can be learned from successful federally sponsored projects, such as NSF's MESA. Focusing on interdisciplinary, action-oriented instructional techniques, MESA improved the mathematics proficiency of minority youth to levels comparable to the majority population. MESA proved that given the opportunity to learn mathematics in a meaningful way, black students can indeed improve their achievement.

School programs and processes and teacher expectations and commitment should be dedicated to providing successful experiences for blacks in mathematics. The effective-schools literature suggests that good leadership that involves faculty in the decision-making process can make a difference in school processes and thus student performance. To this end, educational leaders have a responsibility to change the approach to the secondary-school education of blacks in mathematics.

Responsible leadership must move to implement in-school, MESA-type projects, engaging mathematics faculty and curriculum supervisors in primary leadership roles. Priority should be given to (*a*) revising course experiences so that the focus is on interdisciplinary, action-oriented mathematics; (*b*) providing problem-solving situations involving the study of real-world phenomena; and (*c*) providing activities and instructions that develop higher-order thinking and reasoning skills.

To preserve the democratic ideals of this nation and to produce citizens who are contributors to rather than burdens on society, educators and policymakers must eliminate the historical and psychological barriers to black achievement in mathematics. The processes of academic tracking must be governed by policies that ensure equal access to quality instruction for all students. Academic support structures to sustain the enrollment of black students in quality mathematics courses must be developed consistent with research findings. Advanced courses need to be revised to provide bridging experiences, and innovative strategies for eliminating cumulative pre-algebra deficiencies must be identified. Schools need to adopt policy statements on equity that also encourage the active engagement of all students in classroom activities.

2

Black Participation and Performance
in High School Science

As the United States continues to excel in advanced technology, it is imperative that our educational system graduate scientifically literate citizens. The
future of U.S. technology depends upon young adults adequately trained and
motivated in high school to select science in college and choose it as a career
(Hueftle, Rakow, and Welch 1983). Therefore, our society cannot be content
with a decreasing level of scientific literacy among high school youth or with
the ethnic disparities that now exist in science education (Rakow and Walker
1985; Rakow, Welch, and Hueftle 1984).

The average science achievement test scores of the nation's school-age
population have declined steadily since the early 1960s. This decline is more
marked in the higher grades and for black youth (National Assessment of Educational Progress, 1979b; Jones 1981). In spite of their lag behind the nation
in science achievement, black students continue to exhibit positive attitudes
toward science. Fleming and Malone (1982) state that black elementary
school students are less interested in science when compared to whites, but
the difference dissipates by middle school, and blacks actually have more
favorable attitudes than their white counterparts by high school. However,
according to Kahle (1982), the attitudinal responses of black high school students are generally positive toward science, but these students are also uncertain about the scope and use of science.

As is true for achievement, selection of high school science courses is a
national problem; according to Blosser (1984), approximately 50 percent of
students nationwide take no science after grade ten. Therefore, when these
students take tests during their senior year, they have not been enrolled in a

The significant contributions of Dr. Joan Baratz-Snowden in the preparation of this chapter are
gratefully acknowledged.

science course for two years, and the course they studied probably was biology. Furthermore, Berryman (1983) reports that from the early school years on, poor and minority students receive limited instructional time in mathematics and science and their science career plans are generally less related to their abilities or course-taking behavior. Rakow and Walker (1985) claim that while there is no statistically significant difference in the number of science courses that the majority population and minority students elect to take in high school, there is a statistically significant difference in the number of college preparatory courses for the two groups, with minority students averaging about a third of a semester less than the majority population. Thus, lower enrollments in advanced high school science courses, especially among female and black students (Thomas 1986a; Miller and Remick 1978; Ignatz 1975), do have an impact on their achievement scores and restrict their choices for vocational preparation.

The purpose of this chapter is to describe the present status of blacks in science through the presentation of attitudinal, enrollment, and achievement data in science for black high school students. The data gathered from national testing and assessment programs will be examined to document changes in science achievement and to compare the science achievement and experiences of black high school students to high school students nationally. In addition to these reviews, the chapter will point out the educational implications of the findings.

Data

The data presented in this chapter are from the National Assessment of Educational Progress (NAEP), the Minnesota Science Assessment and Research Project (SARP), High School and Beyond (HSB), and the Admissions Testing Program (ATP).

NAEP, sponsored by the United States Office of Education, has assessed the achievement of American students in science three times: in 1969/1970, in 1972/1973, and in 1976/1977. Science test questions were administered to a nationally representative sample of nine-, thirteen-, and seventeen-year-olds and young adults (age twenty-six to thirty-five). In 1981/1982, SARP conducted a national assessment in science, funded by the National Science Foundation (NSF), which was a modified version of the previous NAEP in science. For this chapter, only the data for thirteen- and seventeen-year-olds are considered to describe changes in black performance between assessments and changes in the group's position compared to the national population. Also, the 1977 and 1982 assessments' findings concerning students' attitudes toward science, science education, scientists, and scientific research will be examined.

The HSB data base, a national longitudinal study, is another resource for systematic examination of secondary education. The science test was given to a national sample of 1980 sophomores and 1982 seniors, and the results provide a basis for describing changes in science performance over the last two years of high school, especially when most students are not taking science courses. This data base also provides information about academic course work and, more specifically, about the science enrollment patterns of high school seniors.

The ATP, a service of the College Board, provides annual summaries of college-bound seniors. The reports provide demographic information as well as Scholastic Aptitude Test (SAT) and Achievement Test (AT) scores of the ethnic, racial, male, and female populations. Variables of interest for this chapter are number of years of study by subject in high school, intended areas of study, and AT scores.

Science Attitudes

The 1976/1977 NAEP Science Assessment investigated attitudes toward science and science education. The attitudinal questions were categorized under three general topics: 1) personal experience with science, 2) science and society, and 3) awareness of the philosophy and methodology of science. "Personal experience with science" refers to feelings about science classes, feelings about science-related careers, experiences with science-related activities, and use of the scientific method of inquiry. Included under "science and society" are confidence in science, support for scientific research, feelings about research on controversial issues, and personal involvement in helping solve science-related societal problems. "Awareness of the philosophy and methodology of science" addresses the understanding of the empirical nature of science, the tentativeness of scientific conclusions, and the function of scientific theories (National Assessment of Educational Progress 1979a).

The data reveal that black high school students like science. They have positive attitudes toward science classes and science-related careers, especially black students in senior high schools (Table 2.1).

However, blacks were not so likely as all students nationwide to report that they had visited places connected with science (e.g., a planetarium, zoo, museum, factory, ocean, electric-generating plant, sewage-treatment plant, scientific laboratory) or had seen various science-related activities firsthand (e.g., a seed sprouting, egg hatching, animal being born, ants or bees working, the North Star, the moon through a telescope, a fossil). Blacks reported fewer science-related experiences and less use of scientific problem-solving methods than the national average, and the disparity increased with age.

TABLE 2.1   Positive Responses to Attitudinal Items

	Personal experiences				Science and society		
	Science classes	Vocational aspirations	Tools and attributes	All experiences	Support research	Personal involvement	Awareness
Age thirteen							
Nation	49.6%	51.9%	64.5%	59.9%	72.1%	53.1%	67.6%
Black	0.6[a]	5.0[a]	−6.1[a]	−2.6[a]	−2.9[a]	−2.0	−6.4[a]
Age seventeen							
Nation	45.7%	48.5%	72.4%	61.4%	77.9%	56.5%	78.1%
Black	5.2[a]	9.1[a]	−9.7[a]	−1.7	−3.1	−2.9	−9.5

SOURCE: National Assessment of Educational Progress 1979.
NOTES: Black percentage differences from the nation, 1976–1977.
[a]Significant difference from national average at the .05 level.

A substantial portion of the blacks did not have confidence in the ability of science to solve most or some of our problems. When asked if science and technology have changed life for better or worse, seventeen-year-old blacks were more likely to report that science had made no changes in their lives or to express no opinion on the subject. Blacks appeared less convinced than students nationally of the benefits of science to society and less supportive of science research. Blacks did not believe so strongly as their national peers that individual actions can make a difference in solving societal problems, and blacks were less willing to perform various conservation and energy-saving activities.

On the average, one-half of the thirteen-year-olds and about two-thirds of the seventeen-year-olds responded in a manner indicating awareness of the assumptions and methods of the scientific process. But blacks at each age level responded significantly below the nation (8 to 11 percentage points) in demonstrating awareness of scientific methods and philosophies. They were least sure about whether scientists believe that all events have causes, were not so certain whether scientists should criticize one another's work, and were less sure that an important use of scientific theories is to predict future events.

SARP conducted the second national survey of students' attitudes toward science in 1982, by which time the overall attitudes among secondary school students declined more than 6 percent but blacks continued to have favorable attitudes toward science. The attitude items of the SARP survey were grouped into three clusters: the first cluster dealt with the behavioral component of attitudes and student activities in science; the second examined attitudes toward science classes, science teachers, science careers, and the value of science; and the third addressed the students' degree of socioscientific responsibility—their willingness to help solve problems and their actual behavior.

In 1982 the participation of thirteen-year-old black males in science-related experiences tended to be near the national average, but by age seventeen, participation in science activities dropped below the national average. Black females of both age groups reported a level of experience below that of the nation as a whole; however, black females made a significant gain between the two assessments.

Thirteen-year-old black males displayed the most positive attitude of all students assessed toward their science classes, science teachers, and the pursuit of a science career; the black females displayed attitudes similar to their national counterparts. When comparing 1982 results to those reported in 1977, the attitudes of the males toward their science teachers rose 10 percentage points. Moreover, compared to the national sample, black thirteen-year-old males consistently expressed a significantly higher interest in science as a career, in both 1977 and 1982.

As was true in 1977, significantly more black seventeen-year-olds in 1982, compared to seventeen-year-olds nationally, held favorable attitudes toward their science classes and science as a career. Blacks averaged 6 percentage points above the national mean for their attitudes toward their science classes and pursuit of a science career. In 1977 black seventeen-year-old students scored well below the national average on the value of science, but in 1982 their responses were close to the national average.

Compared to the nation, black thirteen-year-old students revealed more positive perceptions of their ability and willingness to solve various social problems, as revealed by the 1982 results, while black seventeen-year-olds were near the national average for socioscientific responsibility. By age seventeen, significantly fewer black students felt that they could help solve various science-related social problems. A majority responded that they would be willing to participate in various activities to alleviate societal problems—such as driving or riding in an economy car, separating trash for recycling, or turning off lights—but less than half of the black students reported actually doing these things. Although black high school students were less certain that social problems could be solved, they engaged in more socially constructive activities in 1981/1982 than they did in 1976/1977.

In summary, blacks are interested in science. Responses to the 1977 NAEP and 1982 SARP surveys of attitudes toward science suggest that black high school students have positive attitudes toward science classes, science teachers, science-related careers, and the value of science. However, they have fewer science experiences, find science less useful to the home and family life, and are less aware of scientific methods and how scientists work. According to Kahle (1982), such inconsistencies may be due to the limited exposure of black secondary school students to science activities that would facilitate the formation of attitudes that reflect an understanding of science methodology and technology as well as its potential. Kahle suggests that the responses of black high school students may not reflect their informed attitudes, but rather opinions that they feel they *should* have. Another explanation for their positive attitudes toward science is that blacks tend to have a positive response set. Bachman and O'Malley (1984) found that blacks are more likely than whites to respond at the positive or agreement end of Likert-type scales, but were not able to attribute this black/white difference to differences in academic achievement, educational aspirations, socioeconomic level, or geographical area. However, this notion suggests a need to focus on the causes and underlying meaning of the positive-response style of blacks toward science.

Science Enrollment Patterns

In junior high schools, science is a required course at each grade level. At the senior high level, the number of science courses a student takes depends on state graduation requirements and the student's interest and career plans. Usually, the sequence of course offerings in senior high school consists of biology, chemistry, and physics. For the majority of students who do not plan science careers, biology is the course elected to fulfill the science requirement and is usually taken in the ninth or tenth grade.

Data from the SARP survey reveal that half of the nation's students take no science after grade ten; only 35 percent take courses beyond the traditional biology class usually offered during the sophomore year (Hueftle, Rakow, and Welch 1983). National data also indicate that blacks take fewer science courses and are less likely to be enrolled in college preparatory programs or advanced science courses. Compared to the nation, minority students are electing or are counseled to enroll in many more science courses that are general in nature (Rakow and Walker 1985). Using data from the 1981/1982 SARP study, Rakow and Walker (1985) found that majority students took an average of 3.60 semesters of the traditional college preparatory science sequence (general science, biology, chemistry, and physics), while minority students took only 3.34 semesters—a significant difference.

On average, American high school students take 2.2 years of science, and students who plan to obtain a college degree take about one more year of science than the average student (Peng 1982). Blacks took 2.1 years of science and were less likely to take basic physics and chemistry.

As mentioned earlier, black students do not choose the appropriate high school subjects for entering a science major in college. In a study of 1981/1982 HSB student transcript data to identify course-taking patterns, 20 percent of the black students earned less than one credit in science (National Center for Educational Statistics 1985a). Over half of black high school students earned one or more credits in general life science or general physical science courses and less than one credit in advanced-level science offerings. Only 26 percent of black students were science concentrators or four-year-college bound. Four percent of the black high school science concentrators earned credits in biology, chemistry, physics, and general science courses. The other 22 percent earned credits in advanced life science courses or in advanced physical science courses, in addition to any credits earned in the general life and general physical science courses.

Examining course-taking behavior by curriculum, Ekstrom (1985) found that the two most commonly taken high school science courses were Biology I and Physical Science. In each curriculum blacks were more likely to have taken Biology I and slightly more likely to have taken Physical Science when compared to all students. Black students in each curriculum were more likely to have taken General Science than the nation as a whole. Blacks were less likely to take Chemistry, the second most popular science course for students in the academic curriculum. The science curriculum also included courses—such as Functional Biology or Chemistry/Physics Concepts—that provide a

TABLE 2.2　Years of Science Study

	1981		1982		1983		1984	
	Nation	*Black*	*Nation*	*Black*	*Nation*	*Black*	*Nation*	*Black*
Biological science								
No courses	5.0%	7.5%	4.8%	7.1%	4.6%	6.6%	4.4%	6.2%
One year	60.7	56.9	60.9	57.7	61.5	58.8	61.4	59.1
Two years	26.6	25.0	26.6	24.7	26.4	24.5	26.6	24.7
Three years	5.2	6.7	5.2	6.6	5.0	6.4	5.1	6.5
Four years	1.8	2.8	1.7	2.7	1.7	2.8	1.7	2.6
Five or more years	0.7	1.2	0.7	1.1	0.7	1.0	0.7	1.0
Mean number of years	1.40	1.44	1.40	1.43	1.40	1.43	1.40	1.43
Physical sciences								
No courses	9.1%	12.9%	8.5%	12.3%	7.9%	11.2%	7.5%	10.7%
One year	32.5	40.7	31.7	39.2	31.0	38.6	30.7	38.6
Two years	34.9	29.3	35.4	30.6	36.0	31.4	36.4	31.6
Three years	18.7	12.0	19.4	12.8	20.0	13.8	20.3	14.0
Four years	3.6	3.6	3.8	3.7	3.9	3.6	3.9	3.7
Five or more years	1.2	1.5	1.2	1.5	1.2	1.3	1.2	1.3
Mean number of years	1.79	1.57	1.82	1.61	1.85	1.64	1.86	1.65

SOURCE: College Entrance Examination Board 1982, 1984a, 1984b, 1985.
NOTE: For college-bound seniors.

watered down version of these subjects. Although academic students enrolled in these courses more frequently than students in the other curricula, blacks of every curricula were less likely to take them. Advanced-level science—such as Honors Biology, Chemistry, and Physics—was taken primarily by students who were in the academic curriculum. Approximately 21 percent of all students in the academic track took an advanced or honors course in biology, 8 percent in chemistry, and 8 percent in physics, but for black students the percentages were 11 and 1 percent for these courses, respectively.

Similarly, the trend reported in *Profiles: College-Bound Seniors* (College Entrance Examination Board 1982, 1984a, 1984b), and reflected in Table 2.2, is that black students take fewer science courses, except biological sciences, than do all other students. Moreover, blacks who are planning to attend college are much more likely than students nationally to report courses in neither biological science nor physical science. These data indicate that black students tend to avoid advanced and quantitative science courses.

In sum, the majority of black students have acquired their science knowledge and skills and understanding of the scientific process through basic courses; blacks in the academic curriculum tend to take fewer of the advanced-level science courses desirable for college preparation than do other students in the academic curriculum. Several factors have been identified as reasons for the ethnic gap in enrollment: lower teacher expectation; shortage of role models; stereotyping of science as a white, male domain; differential exposure of science instruction and inappropriate instructional techniques; unequal tracking by teachers and counselors; lack of support from parents and counselors; low self-confidence; the belief that science will not be needed in a future career or the inability to see the relevance of science; and a lack of success in previous science and mathematics courses (Beane 1985; Lockheed et al. 1985; Olstad et al. 1981; Rowe 1977). Young (1981) found that black students are socialized very early to be more affective and service oriented and less analytical and quantitative in their aspirations, which would account for minimal exposure to experiences that build spatial and physical concepts. Subsequently, the negative impact of ethnic and sex stereotyping in regard to science is evident by the time black students enter the sixth grade (Hurd 1982; James and Smith 1985). The result is that the early inequities in science experiences and activities and the limited participation in high school advanced-level courses directly relate both to blacks' achieving at lower levels and to the underrepresentation of blacks in science-related careers.

Science Achievement

Most educators believe that the more exposure students have to science topics, the better they will perform on measurements of science ability and attitude

TABLE 2.3   Science Exposure, Attitudes, and Achievement

	Science experiences (% reporting experience)	Science attitudes (% reporting favorable responses)	Science achievement (% correct)
Age thirteen			
National average	55.2	55.6	55.9
Black males	55.1	59.4	47.9
Black females	52.0	55.5	45.5
Age seventeen			
National average	61.0	57.2	66.0
Black males	58.5	60.4	54.6
Black females	55.6	59.7	52.5

SOURCE: Science Assessment and Research Project.
NOTE: Results of a 1981–1982 assessment of black students.

(Kahle 1982), and positive attitude or interest in science is positively related to achievement in science (Simpson 1978, 1979; Bloom 1976). But data from the NAEP and SARP surveys appear to contradict these assertions (Table 2.3). Blacks displayed positive attitudes but performed below the national average on the cognitive items and were below the national average for science-related experiences.

NAEP measured science knowledge and skills of elementary and secondary school students in 1969/1970, 1972/1973, and 1976/1977. Black students performed well below the national level in each assessment of science achievement; the average percentage of correct responses for blacks ranged from 10 to 16 points below the nation (NAEP 1979b, 1978).

NAEP also reported changes in achievement based on identical sets of exercises administered in at least two assessments. The results revealed national declines in achievement for both ages, with seventeen-year-olds declining more between assessments. Though the achievement of blacks is low nationally, it does not decline disproportionately to the nation. For example, although a comparison of the results of the second and third assessments showed a leveling off of the achievement decline for thirteen-year-olds, black thirteen-year-olds improved in achievement. The change in performance for black seventeen-year-old students was not significant or consistent over time.

Results of the 1982 science assessment indicate that black high school students were still performing well below the national average in the areas of content, inquiry, and technology and society. A comparison of results from the SARP survey conducted in 1981/1982 with those from the 1977 NAEP science assessment revealed a slight decline in science scores among seventeen-year-olds and no significant change for thirteen-year-olds. In contrast to the national trend, the overall scores of blacks of both age groups indicated little change from 1977 to 1982.

On content items (biology, physical science, earth sciences, and integrated topic items), black thirteen-year-old males increased their performance scores from 1977 to 1982, while black seventeen-year-old males and females declined in performance from 1977 to 1982. There was little performance difference in the inquiry areas since 1977 for black students and students nationally at age thirteen. At age seventeen the change in performance for both blacks and all students nationally revealed a serious problem in applying science processes.

Generally, students in 1981/1982 knew less about applications of science research to societal issues than did students in 1976/1977. The results also reveal that black students still performed below the national average on each of the assessments, indicating less understanding of how science influences their lives and the lives of others. However, the thirteen-year-old black males and seventeen-year-old black females did demonstrate small gains between assessments.

HSB data also indicate that the achievement of blacks in science is low nationally. Black high school students tend to score 4 points below the national average. On average, blacks and students nationally showed a slight improvement in science skills over the last two years of high school when contrasting the performance of sophomores and seniors (National Center for Education Statistics 1985b).

When examining data of college-bound seniors, blacks who plan a career in science still performed at least 68 points below the national average on the AT in physics, biology, and chemistry (College Entrance Examination Board 1982, 1984a, 1984b). Furthermore, over the four-year period 1981–1984, blacks slightly improved their scores on the biology achievement test, but performance on the tests in physics and chemistry remained the same.

The evidence indicates that the average performance of black high school students on science achievement tests is below the national average. Performance on several achievement tests indicates little change or only a slight improvement. Olstad et al. (1981) points out that black students performed best on those items most dependent on daily experience and common knowledge and poorest on those which involve a detached research attitude toward the object and phenomena of science. Holmes (1982) reports that early difficulties on test items in biology and physical science may be somewhat ameliorated from ages nine to seventeen. However, early difficulties encountered with science comprehension and application items not only remain but are accentuated with age.

The latest N A E P science assessment (Mullis and Jenkins 1988) reveals that black students have made substantial gains in science achievement but the performance gap relative to white students remains a serious concern. The average science proficiency of black students is at least four years behind that of their white peers. In 1986 only 12 percent of seventeen-year-old blacks demonstrated the ability to analyze scientific procedures and data. Less than one percent of the black students demonstrated the ability to integrate specialized scientific information; that is, most were not able to infer relationships or draw conclusions using detailed scientific knowledge from the physical sciences or apply basic principles to genetics and interpret the social implications of research in ths field. These low percentages are disturbing because the first suggests that a large proportion of black students are not literate about scientific issues and the second projects a dismal picture of the number of high school blacks who have enough talent and understanding of the subject to expect realistically to become scientists.

Implications and Perspectives

This discussion has attempted to present the current status of black high school students in three areas: attitudes toward science, achievement in science, and enrollment in science courses. The current data reveal:

■ Blacks have positive attitudes about science overall. However, these attitudes are in conflict when attitudinal questions are directed at awareness of the philosophy and methodology of science, confidence in science, and science research.

■ Blacks have fewer science-related experiences and less use of scientific problem-solving methods than the national average, and the disparity increases with age.

■ Blacks perform below the national average in science achievement tests. They perform best on questions reflecting daily experience and common knowledge and have difficulty on those which involve comprehension and application of process methods in both biology and physical science.

■ On average, blacks take less than three years of high school science and tend to avoid advanced science courses. Blacks take fewer science courses, except for biological science, than do all other students. Blacks who are college bound are much more likely than their national peers to report no courses in the biological science or physical science areas. Also, those who have considered science as a major are less likely to have taken three or more years of high school science courses.

Overall the data reveal progress, inconsistencies, and disparity. Because of lack of parity for blacks in science careers and inequities in both participation and achievement in science at the high school level, educators and policy-makers must continue to address the issues regarding the relationships among interest or awareness, participation, and performance for minorities in science and how these factors at the high school level affect entry and retention in science work at the postsecondary level. Further exploration is needed to help educators determine how to stimulate enrollment and improve achievement in science by capitalizing on black students' positive perceptions about science classes and science teachers as well as how to institutionalize the successful strategies and techniques utilized in science intervention programs for minority students. There must be home-school-community-wide efforts to raise black students' awareness of how science affects their lives and to increase their understanding of the interaction among science, technology, and society.

The reflections of researchers and the data bases used in this chapter tend to suggest specific positive relationships. Interest in science should lead to greater participation in science activities and higher achievement in science. Greater participation in science activities and advanced-level science courses should lead to improved performance on science assessments and positive science attitudes based on knowledge and experiences rather than opinions. Higher achievement in science should enhance science attitudes and lead to larger enrollment in high school science courses. Though this may be the case for high-ability blacks or blacks involved in science intervention programs, some results for blacks contradict these assertions.

The positive attitudes toward science have not been accompanied by higher achievement levels in science. Again, this issue raises several questions: Does this differential exist for all ability levels of the black segment? What modifications are needed in the instructional approaches to help black students acquire more than science facts or basic science concepts and rid minority students of the stereotype of science as a white male domain? What are the effective strategies that improve attitudes as well as increase cognitive learning? What are the information-processing similarities and differences among black students of perceiving, acquiring, and using science knowledge?

It is, however, the difficulty with science methodology items that is a problem for both the attitudinal and cognitive analyses. School administrators, science teachers, minority science professionals, and parents must take action to change the fact that the majority of black high school students do not understand science methodology, its technology, and its potentials (Kahle 1980). Action must be taken to find ways to change the NAEP findings that black students report fewer science experiences, find science less useful out of school, and are less aware of scientific methods and of how scientists work. The results suggest that if educators help black students incorporate the science process into their out-of-school life on a consistent basis, there will be improvement in both their attitudes toward the potential of science and their understanding of the science process, as reflected in comprehension and application test items. James and Smith (1985) contend that cleverly conceived, well prepared, adequately equipped, and properly supervised science experiences can improve students' attitudes toward science as well as their science achievement.

Research is still needed to address a question raised by Berryman (1983): Are there causal relationships between interest and abilities, and do these relationships change depending on the stages of the educational process? She suggests that if interests drive skills, then the focus of intervention should be early career exposure. On the other hand, if skills drive interests, then early interventions should stress scientific and mathematical skills. Both processes are operating during the high school years; however, there is a need to understand better how these processes affect minority students of varying social and educational backgrounds.

While black students' attitudes toward science may be positive, they may not take advanced science courses, for several reasons that have been identified for ethnic disparity in science study. Malcom (1983) points out that all students are adversely affected by inadequate facilities, lack of laboratories and instrumentation, declining numbers of qualified teachers, fewer advanced mathematics and science classes, lack of in-service training opportunities for teachers, curricula that have not kept pace with new technologies or the progress of science, and poor counseling. Moreover, Malcom emphasizes that the education system has traditionally delivered poorer training and even less motivation to minority students: where expectations and attitudes of teachers and counselors are not supportive of the aspirations of minority students in science and mathematics; where the behavior of teachers toward minority students discourages them from classroom participation; where there is differential access to instrumentation and educational technologies; and where minorities are still counseled away from science and technical careers. To eliminate these educational barriers and promote equity for minority students in science, programs are needed to enhance the instructional skills and educational expectations of junior and senior high school science teachers.

Several educational practices—such as curriculum tracking, in-class ability grouping, and differential teacher interaction in science classes—must be eliminated in order to increase science participation and performance. For example, minority women scientists indicated small classes and an early start in the prerequisite courses (which enabled them later to select and succeed in advanced courses) as the most significant factors contributing to their decision to enroll in advanced classes in high school (Beane 1985). Hence teachers— black and white—must provide appealing, investigative science projects and demand high performance from all black students as well as encourage capable black students to take high school mathematics and science courses.

Additionally, science programs should be structured to increase students' confidence in their academic abilities and their potential for excelling in science; black students should be internally motivated and should develop the ability to persevere when faced with a challenge. Black students need classroom experiences that promote realistic goal setting, personal responsibility, and an awareness of personal causation; that allow students sufficient time to think before answering questions; and that require students to hypothesize cause-and-effect relationships (Olstad et al. 1981; Rowe 1977).

Not only do black high school students have problems with analyzing scientific procedures and data, they also experience great difficulty with physical science items. This is not surprising since many black high school students do not enroll in advanced-level or quantitative science courses and since the last science course is usually General Biology or Biology I. Therefore, since the achievement tests are heavily laden with physics and chemistry, blacks must be counseled or motivated to take advanced courses in science.

One issue to be addressed is that not only have enrollments in most science courses declined but what was taught was often diluted (Ekstrom 1985). In addition to increasing the *number* of courses, policymakers must also be concerned about the *type* and *quality*. Courses should not be watered down to allow students to pass the numerical requirements at the expense of achievement in science, and thereby not increase the problem of a science-illiterate citizenry.

Another explanation for consideration when examining achievement and course enrollment relates to the stages of intellectual development. Levine and Lin (1976) state that instruction will not "provoke" the learner unless it is related to the learner's current level of development as characterized by Jean Piaget. Not all adolescents exhibit formal operations when trying to solve logical problems. Renner and Lawson (1983) claim that from 40 to 75 percent of secondary school students have failed to reach the level of formal thought. That is, they cannot do proportional thinking, combinatorial thinking, or solve problems requiring separation and control of variables. If the Piagetian model is correct in contending that concrete thinkers cannot develop understanding of abstract subject matter, and if, indeed, a large portion of secondary school students are performing at concrete operational levels, then a major portion of today's secondary school science curricula is beyond the students' level of understanding and, therefore, inappropriate. Thus, when minority students are confronted with material that is beyond their intellectual level, and if, indeed, they have fewer science experiences, it is inevitable that the outcome will be poor performance and a damaged self-image.

As a result of being exposed to abstract materials before having concepts taught in more concrete form, minority students most often memorize facts without understanding concepts. Minority students experience great difficulty comprehending abstract scientific concepts and lag in building understanding through experiences and observation. Therefore, educators must adhere to Gordon's (1986) suggestion of exposure early in the life of the child (before high school) to hands-on experiences in mathematics, science, and technology, with ample opportunities for exploring, discovering, and questioning relationships between concepts and materials.

Minority students are heavily concentrated in low-income areas and urban schools. NAEP data indicate that students from urban schools perform more poorly on science achievement items than do groups from other segments of society. Minority and disadvantaged students in these areas are often confronted with poorly maintained and poorly equipped science laboratories and have less access to computers. Under these conditions there is often underutilization of the personal, active, and interactive teaching style found to be especially effective with minority students (Beane 1985; Lockheed et al. 1985).

The problem is further compounded when these students are taught by teachers who are not highly motivated, have inadequate knowledge of black achievement in science and engineering, lack adequate science training, have no confidence in their ability to teach it, and do not like science. Minority students will not only perform poorly but will be turned off by inadequate facilities and the anxiety-avoidance syndrome of teachers. Policymakers and administrators must reconcile this imbalance of both human and material resources between the privileged and the underprivileged. Additionally, Wirszup (1983) highlights the need to encourage institutions of higher learning and their colleges of education to reevaluate their activities and to assume new responsibilities and commitment with regard to high-quality teacher-training programs and the establishment of close working ties with elementary and secondary schools in promoting science literacy.

Low achievement in science does seem to be related to decreasing enrollment in science and to differential treatment. This suggests that strategies must be employed to increase the participation of blacks—regardless of ability—in science courses in order that higher achievement levels (at least comparable to the national average) become an attainable goal. Students who excel in science usually have a background that includes three or four years of high school mathematics and science. Evidence has shown that inadequate mathematical preparation is detrimental to success in such advanced, quantitative science courses as physics and chemistry. More research is needed to determine what factors affect black students' decisions to choose lower-level courses and to identify those practices which promote participation in advanced science courses. It is to be hoped that, with the national recommendation (National Commission on Excellence in Education 1983) to increase the number of mathematics and science courses required of students, the increased participation will be accompanied by improved achievement scores.

3

Black Science Majors
in Colleges and Universities

This chapter presents national data describing the enrollment and degree-completion status of black students in mathematics and science majors in U.S. colleges and universities. The availability of data to assess the recent progress of blacks in natural and technical science fields is essential for two reasons. First, blacks have traditionally and persistently been underrepresented in majors and careers in the natural and technical sciences (Malcom, Hall, and Brown 1976; Thomas 1980; Trent 1984; Vetter and Babco 1986). As a result, various efforts have been initiated by the federal government and other organizations to increase the participation of black students in mathematics and science majors and careers (Bromery 1981; Garrison 1985; Melnick and Hamilton 1981; Richards, Williams, and Holland 1981). Therefore, data on the enrollment and degree-completion status of blacks in higher education should be useful in assessing the extent to which the goals of these programs have been achieved.

Second, the current shift in the U.S. economy and labor market to highly technological jobs will require that all Americans acquire more extensive and higher-order analytical skills to assume high-tech jobs (National Science Board Commission on Precollege Education in Mathematics, Science, and Technology 1984). Thus it becomes important to increase as well as monitor the progress of groups that have been traditionally underrepresented in scientific and technical majors and careers. Goldman and Hewitt (1986, 50) noted that "scientists and engineers exert considerable influence on U.S. society, and therefore any group that contributes few scientists and engineers is at least partly disenfranchised." Also, data collected and reported by the College

This research was supported by grants from the Spencer Foundation and the Rockefeller Foundation. Special thanks are extended to Linda Jackson for her invaluable assistance in collecting and preparing data for this chapter.

Placement Council (1982) indicate that college graduates in natural and technical science majors are more successful in obtaining employment and higher salaries than college graduates in education and the social sciences (fields that blacks have traditionally pursued).

This chapter will focus on black underrepresentation in mathematics and science and present the most reliable data from the Office of Civil Rights (OCR) available at the time of this inquiry. OCR data on black student enrollments in mathematics and science for the fall of 1982 and degree-completion data in these fields for 1980/1981 are presented. In some instances comparable data will be presented for whites to assess the progress of blacks in these fields relative to whites. Also, institutional-level data will be presented to determine the extent to which various colleges and universities have been productive in enrolling and graduating black undergraduates and graduate students in selected majors in the natural and technical sciences. Finally, the implications of the findings and alternatives for increasing the participation of blacks will be discussed.

Underrepresentation in Math and Science

In 1980 blacks were approximately 12 percent of the U.S. population, but only 10.3 percent of the nation's four-year-college enrollees, 6.5 percent of the nation's four-year-college graduates, 5.8 percent of its master's degree recipients, and 3.9 percent of its doctoral degree recipients (U.S. Office of Civil Rights 1981). In the natural and technical sciences (engineering, mathematics, and the physical and biological sciences) blacks were severely underrepresented among graduate degree recipients at the master's and doctoral levels relative to their representation in the college-age population and their representation among four-year-college degree holders.

Blacks were also highly underrepresented among employed natural and technical scientists relative to white males and females and relative to their representation among advanced-degree holders (master's and doctoral degree recipients). For example, unpublished data by the Bureau of Labor Statistics (Vetter and Babco 1986) showed that blacks were only 2.6 percent of the nation's employed engineers, 2.9 percent of employed mathematicians, 1.5 percent of employed physical scientists, and only 1.6 percent of the nation's employed biological and life scientists. Previous and more recent studies have offered a number of explanations regarding the underrepresentation of blacks in natural and technical science majors and careers.

Stereotypical and traditional values transmitted by the family, school, and broader society have been identified as important factors that shape and limit the educational and career expectations of blacks. Historically, pursuing mathematics and science majors and careers has been viewed as more appropriate for males than for females and more for whites than for blacks. Conversely, social and service-oriented careers have been viewed as more appropriate for minorities (Klein and Bailey 1975; Maccoby and Jacklin 1974). Malcom, Hall, and Brown (1976) noted that minority women scientists who were successful in overcoming traditional race and sex stereotypes and barriers were often confronted by their families and friends with traditional expectations and values, and were not encouraged by their teachers and counselors to pursue nontraditional careers.

Many black students do not have the type of family-support networks and role models that would facilitate their access to science and mathematics majors and careers. Malcom, Hall, and Brown (1976) and Pearson and Pearson (1985) noted that the majority of the nation's black scientists were first-generation scientists with very few role models or "significant others" (i.e., parents, teachers, and peers) to encourage them and to facilitate their success. Also, Crain and Mahard (1978) found that the lower the proportion of black teachers in secondary schools and the lower the degree of interaction of black students with black teachers, the lower black students' high school grade performance and college attendance. Blackwell (1981) reported a similar finding regarding the positive influence of black faculty presence on the enrollment and retention of black students. Thus having access to black professional role models and receiving encouragement and sponsorship from these individuals to pursue advanced degrees—especially in the natural and technical sciences—are critical for black students.

The personal values, interests, and career expectations of minorities also influence their participation in mathematics and science majors and careers. Hager and Elton (1971) reported that the black high school students in their sample expressed greater interest than whites in artistic, health, social, business, and clerical careers and less interest than whites in technical and scientific careers. Thomas's 1984 survey of the major field choice and career interests of a sample of black and white college seniors indicated similar results. Studies also suggest that many black students do not see the utility or relevancy of careers in mathematics and science to their daily lives (Matthews 1983). Finally, Chipman and Thomas (1984) noted that many minority students have not received adequate professional socialization to pursue and complete majors and careers in mathematics and science. As a result, some of these students are either not willing or not prepared to pursue the long hours that mathematics and science homework and laboratory projects require. Studies also show that although black students express similar levels of interest and affinity in mathematics and sciences as whites, they spend less time on mathematics and science homework than do whites (Chipman and Thomas 1984; Thomas 1984).

Gaining access to higher education and obtaining adequate financial aid to pursue college majors in mathematics and science are two critical barriers for black students. Below national average performance on standardized tests required for college and subsequent higher education entry remains a major inhibiting factor for most black students. For example, although black students improved their performance on the Scholastic Aptitude Test (SAT) between 1981 and 1983, neither black males nor black females averaged a total score (mathematics and verbal combined) of 800 on the SAT during these time periods (Thomas 1986b). The maximum score on the mathematics and verbal portions of the SAT combined is 1600 (a maximum of 800 on each component).

Similar to the SAT, the maximum score on the mathematics and verbal portions of the Graduate Record Examination (GRE) is 1600 (a maximum of 800 on each section). A study by the Educational Testing Service (ETS) reported that only 2.4 percent of the black male and female GRE test takers scored above 600 on the quantitative section of the test, as compared to 22 percent and 20 percent respectively for white GRE test takers (Flamer, Horch, and Davis 1982). However, 1982/1983 data from the GRE for black undergraduate test takers by major field showed that black majors in the natural and technical sciences (biology, mathematics, engineering, and the physical sciences) scored about 800 on the GRE and exceeded the test performance of the average black test taker. During this period, black undergraduate test takers in biology obtained an average score of 825 (1117 for whites); in mathematics black undergraduates scored an average of 857 (1219 for whites); in engineering black undergraduates scored an average of 1015 (1222 for whites); and in the physical sciences black undergraduates scored an average of 888 on the GRE (1172 for whites).

Securing adequate financial aid, particularly given the increase in tuition at most college and universities, is also a problem for many black students (Copeland 1984). Thomas (1981) found that if having high family resources and financial aid were the major requirements for four-year-college access, then only 16 percent of the black respondents in the 1972 National Longitudinal Survey of High School Seniors would have attended college as opposed to the 31 percent who actually did attend. Because the cost of graduate education is greater than that of undergraduate education, obtaining graduate degrees in the natural and technical sciences is an even greater challenge for economically disadvantaged black students. In 1980 graduate and professional students borrowed approximately $1.3 billion in private capital through the Graduate Student Loan (GSL) Program (Flamer, Horch, and Davis 1982). Although heavy borrowing and reliance on loans are increasingly characteristic of students who pursue higher education, black students have a strong bias against obtaining educational loans because of extensive family and financial obligations (Cross and Astin 1981). Chipman and Thomas (1984) noted that supplemental aid in the form of grants rather than loans and work-study are important, especially for minority mathematics and science majors who need money to purchase laboratory equipment and adequate time for laboratory and computer projects.

Institutional recruitment practices and discrimination also influence the enrollment and participation of black students and other minorities in mathematics and science. Copeland (1984) reported that despite the below-national-average performance of blacks on standardized achievement tests, most of the leading colleges and universities still target their recruitment efforts to the limited number of blacks who perform above average on these tests. At the same time, admission officers and affirmative action personnel at these institutions report that they are committed to increasing equality of educational opportunity and their enrollment of black and minority students (Copeland 1984). In addition, a study by the Council of Graduate Schools in the U.S. (1984) reported that graduate schools (especially in the arts and sciences) were less likely to have recruitment and academic assistance and tutorial programs for minorities than were professional schools (those with programs in law and medicine). Structural discrimination and biases from peers, teachers, and employers also have been cited as factors that discourage the participation of minorities in mathematics and science. Malcom, Hall, and Brown (1976) and Chipman and Thomas (1984) noted that minority scientists are often confronted with hostile work environments and are excluded from full participation in the formal and informal networks and activities in their professions. Chipman and Thomas also noted that some nationally sponsored workshops and special high school programs in physics and in science and technology were traditionally not open to women and disadvantaged minorities. Cole (1981) contends that such exclusionary processes create additional barriers for minorities.

Black Participation in Mathematics and Science

As previously noted, a variety of efforts have been pursued in the 1980s to increase the participation of blacks, women, and other minorities in mathematics and science. Given these efforts, it would be useful to determine the current status of higher education enrollment and degree completion of black students in these fields. The remainder of this chapter will address the question by providing national and institutional data on black enrollment and degree completion. The OCR survey data upon which this inquiry is based was initially conducted in 1968 and has been repeated biennially since. Student enrollment and degree-completion data by race, sex, and college major are included in the survey and are collected from all federally funded colleges and universities—over 3,000 institutions.

The OCR data have been used primarily for governmental reporting and monitoring purposes to determine the progress of various public institutions in enrolling and retaining women and racial minorities. These data are routinely reported in statistical documents by the National Center for Education and the American Council on Education for purposes of providing tabular summary reports to the public. However, the data are seldom employed in descriptive studies that highlight the research, policy, and educational implications of the data regarding minorities. This is the primary contribution and uniqueness of this study.

Findings

Tables 3.1 and 3.2 present national data on the undergraduate and graduate enrollment and degree attainment of black and white males and females in the biological sciences, engineering, mathematics, and the physical sciences.

Table 3.1 reports the undergraduate (two-year and four-year combined) and graduate enrollments of black and white males and females in the biological sciences, engineering, mathematics, and the physical sciences in 1982. Four-year- and two-year-college enrollment data by field of study were not reported separately by OCR. The highest undergraduate enrollments of blacks in the fields shown in Table 3.1 were in mathematics (9.8 percent) and the biological sciences (8.3 percent), while their lowest enrollments in 1982 were in the physical sciences (4.6 percent) and engineering (5.0 percent). Table 3.1 also shows that in most instances, black male and female undergraduates were almost equally distributed in mathematics and the physical sciences in 1982. However, black female undergraduate enrollment in the biological sciences exceeded black male enrollment by 2 percent, while black male undergraduate enrollment in engineering exceeded black female enrollment by 2 percent. In contrast, white males exceeded white females in undergraduate enrollment in all four fields shown in Table 3.1, with sex differences most pronounced among whites in engineering and the physical sciences. Also, sex disparities favoring males in undergraduate enrollment in the natural and technical science fields in Table 3.1 were much greater among whites than among blacks in 1982.

The graduate enrollment distributions for blacks in the natural and

TABLE 3.1 Enrollments in Undergraduate and Graduate Institutions

Undergraduate

Groups	Biological Sciences		Engineering		Mathematics		Physical Sciences	
	N	%	N	%	N	%	N	%
Blacks	13,494	8.3	19,379	5.0	5,393	9.8	4,514	4.6
Males	5,035	3.1	13,772	3.6	2,694	4.9	2,498	2.5
Females	8,459	5.2	5,607	1.4	2,699	4.9	2,016	2.1
Whites	131,487	80.4	307,838	79.6	44,371	80.7	84,645	85.9
Males	68,657	42.0	263,073	68.0	24,874	45.2	62,755	63.7
Females	62,830	38.4	44,765	11.6	19,497	35.5	21,890	22.2
Total[a]	163,473	100.0	389,910	100.0	54,979	100.0	98,528	100.0
Males	83,491	51.1	328,749	85.0	30,747	55.9	71,924	73.0
Females	79,982	48.9	58,161	15.0	24,232	44.1	26,604	27.0

Graduate

Groups	Biological Sciences		Engineering		Mathematics		Physical Sciences	
	N	%	N	%	N	%	N	%
Blacks	595	2.5	458	1.2	93	1.4	307	1.2
Males	293	1.2	363	1.0	54	.8	225	.9
Females	302	1.3	95	.2	39	.6	82	.3
Whites	19,205	80.5	18,555	49.7	3,603	55.8	17,870	70.9
Males	11,561	48.5	15,875	42.5	2,506	38.8	14,072	55.8
Females	7,644	32.0	2,680	7.2	1,097	17.0	3,798	15.1
Total	23,847	100.0	37,362	100.0	6,453	100.0	25,216	100.0
Males	14,422	60.5	33,425	89.5	4,664	72.3	20,055	79.5
Females	9,425	39.5	3,973	10.5	1,789	27.7	5,161	20.5

NOTES: Total full-time, by race, sex, and field, for the nation (fall 1982). Undergraduates included two-year and four-year college enrollees. [a]Groups other than blacks and whites included in the total are Native Americans, Alaskan natives, Hispanic-Americans, Asians, and nonresident aliens.

TABLE 3.2   Bachelors', Masters', and Doctors' Degrees Awarded

| | Biological sciences | | | | | | Engineering | | | | | |
| | Bachelors | | Masters | | Doctorate | | Bachelors | | Masters | | Doctorate | |
Groups	N	%	N	%	N	%	N	%	N	%	N	%
Blacks	2,266	5.2	171	2.9	64	1.7	2,432	3.3	260	1.6	24	.9
Males	951	2.2	82	1.4	36	.9	2,003	2.7	222	1.4	23	.9
Females	1,315	3.0	89	1.5	28	.8	429	.6	38	.2	1	—
Whites	37,232	86.3	5,209	87.2	3,177	85.4	60,066	81.1	10,147	62.0	1,352	53.0
Males	21,049	48.8	3,223	53.9	2,288	61.5	53,694	72.5	9,177	56.1	1,296	50.8
Females	16,183	37.5	1,986	33.3	889	23.9	6,372	8.6	970	5.9	56	2.2
Totals[a]	43,166	100.0	5,977	100.0	3,718	100.0	74,092	100.0	16,358	100.0	2,551	100.0
Males	24,107	55.8	3,654	61.1	2,666	71.7	64,417	89.6	14,998	91.7	2,447	95.9
Females	19,059	44.2	2,323	38.9	1,052	28.3	7,675	10.4	1,360	8.3	104	4.1

| | Mathematics | | | | | | Physical sciences | | | | | |
| | Bachelors | | Masters | | Doctorate | | Bachelors | | Masters | | Doctorate | |
Groups	N	%	N	%	N	%	N	%	N	%	N	%
Blacks	582	5.3	67	2.6	9	1.2	886	3.8	107	2.0	32	1.0
Males	274	2.5	33	1.3	6	.8	593	2.5	79	1.5	28	.9
Females	308	2.8	34	1.3	3	.4	293	1.3	28	.5	4	.1
Whites	9,353	85.2	1,890	73.7	507	69.6	20,958	88.8	4,115	78.7	2,445	77.9
Males	5,335	48.6	1,212	47.2	422	58.0	15,853	67.1	3,255	62.3	2,153	68.6
Females	4,018	36.6	678	26.5	85	11.6	5,105	21.7	860	16.4	292	9.3
Totals[a]	10,982	100.0	2,565	100.0	728	100.0	23,610	100.0	5,227	100.0	3,140	100.0
Males	6,251	56.9	1,690	65.9	614	84.3	17,742	75.1	4,144	79.3	2,764	88.0
Females	4,731	43.1	875	34.1	114	15.7	5,868	24.9	1,083	20.7	376	12.0

Notes: Degrees in the natural and technical sciences by race and sex in institutions of higher education, 1980–1981.
[a] Totals include Hispanic-Americans, Native Americans, Alaskan natives, Asian-Americans, and nonresident aliens in addition to blacks and whites.

technical sciences in Table 3.1 indicate that blacks were severely underrepresented in enrollment at the graduate level in 1982 compared to the enrollment of black undergraduates. Graduate enrollment underrepresentation in the four fields shown in Table 3.1 was greatest for blacks in mathematics and the physical sciences. Whites were also severely underrepresented in both mathematics and engineering compared to their enrollment at the undergraduate level. The low representation of white graduate students in mathematics and engineering has been attributed to the high graduate enrollment and degree attainment of nonresident aliens in programs in the natural and technical sciences in U.S. graduate programs (Berryman 1983; Thomas 1986b).

Table 3.1 shows that the greatest enrollment concentration of blacks and whites in graduate programs among the four fields shown was in the biological sciences. Whites were 80 percent of the graduate student enrollments in the biological sciences. This was equivalent to their enrollment representation in the biological sciences at the undergraduate level. Blacks were 2.5 percent of the graduate enrollments in the biological sciences, but less than 1.5 percent of the graduate enrollments in engineering, mathematics, and the physical sciences in 1982.

Table 3.2 presents data on undergraduate and graduate degrees conferred on blacks and whites in the natural and technical sciences in 1980/1981. The most obvious finding from these data is that the degree-attainment rates of both groups clearly decrease as the level of educational attainment increases. Thus the attrition of students, especially blacks, throughout the educational pipeline noted by Astin (1982) is quite apparent in the OCR data for 1980/1981. The one exception to this pattern is among whites in the biological sciences, where their degree-attainment rate is about equal at the undergraduate and graduate levels (85 and 87 percent, respectively). There is a drastic decline for whites in degree attainment in engineering, mathematics, and the physical sciences relative to their undergraduate enrollment and degree attainment in these fields. However, again, this has been attributed to the high levels of enrollments and degree attainment of nonresident aliens in master's and doctoral programs in these fields in colleges and universities (Berryman 1983; Thomas 1986a). Despite their underrepresentation in degree attainment in these fields at the graduate level, whites were far more likely than blacks (seventeen to eighteen times more likely) to be represented among doctoral degree recipients in the natural and technical sciences.

OCR data reveal that despite various efforts to increase black participation in the natural and technical sciences, blacks remain severely underrepresented at the undergraduate and graduate levels in enrollment and degree attainment in the biological sciences, mathematics, the physical sciences, and in engineering in the decade of the 1980s. To the extent that blacks obtained degrees in these fields during this time, they did so primarily at the baccalaureate level. However, even at this level, blacks were far more underrepresented than whites in these fields (although whites also experienced some underrepresentation—primarily at the graduate level in mathematics and engineering).

An examination of sex differences indicated that at both the undergraduate and graduate levels, black female enrollment and degree attainment in the biological sciences and mathematics was almost equivalent to that of black males. However, black females were far less represented than black males in undergraduate and graduate degree attainment in the physical sciences and engineering. In contrast, white females were at a much greater disadvantage than black females relative to their male counterparts in undergraduate and graduate enrollment and degree attainment in all of the fields examined.

The previous data provided a national picture of the status of black student enrollment and degree attainment in the natural and technical sciences. The remaining data presented will be for the institutional level. These data will permit an assessment of the contribution of predominantly black and other institutions to the pool of black degree recipients in these fields.

Jay (1971) conducted a study of the baccalaureate origins of black scientists (biological scientists, chemists, physical scientists, pharmaceutical scientists, and agricultural scientists) for a 1958 and a 1960–1969 cohort of black scientists. Among the 1958 sample, 72 percent had received their undergraduate degrees from traditionally black institutions, and the ten leading institutions that awarded baccalaureate degrees to these black scientists were also traditionally black colleges and universities. These institutions included Howard University, Morehouse College, Fisk University, Tuskegee Institute, Southern University, Texas Southern, Lincoln University (Pa.), Virginia State College, Hampton Institute, Prairie View A. and M. University, and Talladega College. Jay also reported that the ten leading institutions that awarded baccalaureate degrees to his sample of 1960–1969 black scientists were traditionally black institutions.

Pearson and Pearson (1985) conducted a similar study of the origins of black scientists and also found that the traditionally black colleges played a major role. Two-thirds of the black scientists in their study received their undergraduate degrees from traditionally black colleges. The leading institutions in this study were Howard, Morehouse, Tuskegee, Fisk, Southern, and Texas Southern (a subset of the institutions identified earlier by Jay in 1971).

The remaining data permit a more recent assessment of the progress of predominantly black and other colleges and universities in producing black degree recipients in the natural and technical sciences. The present findings can be compared with the findings in Jay's 1971 study, which were based on data collected prior to higher education desegregation.

In 1972 the *Adams* decision mandated the desegregation of state-supported colleges and universities. Prior to *Adams,* the nation's black colleges and universities educated virtually all blacks who went to college. Currently, however, these institutions enroll less than one-third of the black students in higher education (Garibaldi 1984; National Advisory Committee on Black Higher Education and Black Colleges and Universities 1982).

Table 3.3 shows the contribution of traditionally black institutions (TBIS) and other institutions to the pool of black degree recipients in the natural and technical sciences. In all, 549 institutions awarded a total of 2,255 bachelors' degrees to blacks in the biological sciences. These institutions represented 45 percent of all institutions ($N = 1,222$) that awarded bachelor's degrees in biology to the nation's four-year-college students. Among the 549 institutions that awarded bachelors' degrees to blacks in biology, only 14 percent were TBIS; however, these institutions awarded 40 percent of the bachelors' degrees in biology that blacks received in 1980/1981.

Although the TBIS were only about 10 percent of the institutions that awarded bachelors' degrees to black students in engineering in 1980/1981, they accounted for 35 percent of the total number of bachelors' degrees awarded to blacks in engineering. The contribution of the TBIS to the pool of black bachelors' degree recipients in the natural and technical sciences was even greater in mathematics. These institutions awarded 51 percent of the bachelors' degrees in mathematics that black college students received in 1980/1981. The TBIS were only 22 percent of the nation's institutions that awarded bachelors' degrees to black students in the physical sciences; however, they accounted for approximately 40 percent of the bachelors' degrees that blacks received in the physical sciences.

Table 3.3 shows the role of TBIS and other institutions in awarding masters' degrees to black students in the natural and technical sciences. Although TBIS represented only 15 to 20 percent of the institutions that awarded masters' degrees to blacks in the biological sciences, mathematics, and the physical sciences, they awarded over one-third of the masters' degrees that black students earned in the biological sciences, about one-third of the degrees that blacks earned in mathematics, and almost 40 percent of the masters' degrees that black students earned in the physical sciences. Engineering is the only field shown in Table 3.3 in which the TBIS did not contribute substantially to the pool of masters' degree recipients.

Table 3.3 shows the percent of contribution of the TBIS and other institutions to the limited pool of black doctoral recipients in the natural and technical sciences. Nationally, black Ph.D. recipients were less than 2 percent of the doctoral pool in the biological sciences in 1980/1981, only one percent in the physical sciences, and less than one percent in engineering and mathematics (see Table 3.2). Table 3.3 shows that with the exception of the biological

TABLE 3.3   The Role of Institutions in Awarding Degrees

	Biological sciences		Engineering		Mathematics		Physical sciences	
	N	%	N	%	N	%	N	%
Bachelors' degrees								
Total conferred to blacks	2,266	100.0	2,432	100.0	582	100.0	886	100.0
	(N=549)[a]	(100.0)	(N=263)	(100.0)	(N=230)	(100.0)	(N=287)	(100.0)
Total conferred by TBIs[b]	894	39.5	845	34.7	297	51.0	350	39.5
	(N=78)	(14.2)	(N=26)	(9.9)	(N=71)	(30.9)	(N=63)	(22.0)
Total conferred by other institutions	1,372	60.5	1,587	65.3	285	49.0	536	60.5
	(N=471)	(85.8)	(N=237)	(90.1)	(N=159)	(69.1)	(N=224)	(78.0)
Masters' degrees								
Total conferred to blacks	171	100.0	260	100.0	67	100.0	107	100.0
	(N=90)	(100.0)	(N=83)	(100.0)	(N=48)	(100.0)	(N=60)	(100.0)
Total conferred by TBIs	62	36.3	23	8.8	21	31.3	42	39.3
	(N=15)	(16.7)	(N=3)	(3.6)	(N=7)	(14.6)	(N=12)	(20.0)
Total conferred by other institutions	107	63.7	237	91.2	46	68.7	65	60.7
	(N=75)	(83.3)	(N=80)	(96.4)	(N=41)	(85.4)	(N=48)	(80.0)
Doctoral degrees								
Ph.D.s conferred to blacks	64	100.0	24	100.0	9	100.0	32	100.0
	(N=33)	(100.0)	(N=17)	(100.0)	(N=9)	(100.0)	(N=21)	(100.0)
Ph.D.s conferred by TBIs	21	32.8	0[c]	0	0	0	0	0
	(N=3)	(9.1)						
Ph.D.s conferred by other institutions	43	67.2	24	100.0	9	100.0	32	100.0
	(N=30)	(90.9)	(N=17)	(100.0)	(N=9)	(100.0)	(N=21)	(100.0)

NOTES: Degrees in the natural and technical sciences awarded to blacks, by type of institution, 1980–1981.
[a](N) = institutions that awarded degrees to blacks.
[b]TBIs = traditionally black institutions.
[c]No TBIs awarded doctoral degrees in these fields, 1980–1981.

sciences, institutions other than T B I s (i.e., primarily predominantly white institutions) were the prime contributors (100 percent) to the limited pool of
black doctorates in the natural and technical sciences. This is not surprising
given that the majority of the T B I s (over 99 percent) do not have doctoral
programs in the natural and technical sciences (Garibaldi 1984). However, in
the biological sciences, the T B I s contributed 33 percent to the pool of black
doctorates in 1980/1981, despite their minuscule representation (only three
T B I s among Ph.D.-granting institutions in biology).

The data in Table 3.3 clearly indicate that despite higher education desegregation and the resulting decline in black student enrollment in the nation's
T B I s, these institutions continue to play a major role in the degree attainment
of black students in the natural and technical sciences. The contribution of
these institutions in these fields was especially substantial at the baccalaureate
and master's degree levels. Studies by Garibaldi (1984) and Hill (1984) indicate that the nation's T B I s continue to assume a critical role in the higher education of black students in general. Also, the studies by Jay (1971) and
Pearson and Pearson (1984) showed that these institutions had an even greater
role in contributing to the production of black scientists prior to higher education desegregation.

The final three tables in this chapter (Tables 3.4, 3.5, and 3.6) identify by
name the leading institutions in awarding baccalaureate, masters', and doctoral degrees to black students in the natural and technical sciences. These
tables also show the contributions of leading institutions to their respective
states in producing black degree recipients in these fields. The T B I s are noted
by an asterisk in each of the tables.

Table 3.4 shows the top five institutions in producing black bachelor's degree recipients in the natural and technical sciences in 1980/1981. These data
reveal that in the biological sciences, engineering, and the physical sciences,
all but one of the top five institutions that awarded bachelors' degrees to
blacks in these fields were traditionally black institutions. The City University
of New York (C U N Y)—a predominantly white institution (P W I)—was also
among the top five institutions that awarded bachelors' degrees to black students in the biological sciences and engineering in 1980/1981. Embry-Riddle,
another P W I, was also among the top five institutions that awarded bachelors'
degrees to blacks in the physical sciences during this period. However, in
mathematics, all five of the leading institutions that awarded bachelors' degrees to black students were T B I s.

Table 3.4 shows that many of the leading institutions made a substantial
contribution to their state's production of black bachelor's degree recipients in
the natural and technical sciences in 1980/1981. The most outstanding institutions in this regard were Howard University in the biological sciences; North

TABLE 3.4   Bachelors' Degrees Awarded to Blacks

Institution	$N1^a$	State		$N2^a$	Percent
Biological sciences					
Howard U.*	78^b	D.C.	$(8)^c$	109	71.6
Tenn. State*	43	Tenn.	(35)	115	37.4
CUNY-City	42	N.Y.	(95)	213	19.7
S.C. State*	32	S.C.	(26)	92	34.8
Morehouse*	32	Ga.	(34)	138	23.2
Engineering					
Prairie View*	153	Tex.	(25)	243	62.0
Southern U.*	107	La.	(12)	168	63.7
N.C. A. & T.*	106	N.C.	(6)	150	70.7
CUNY-City	79	N.Y.	(28)	205	38.5
Univ. of D.C.*	70	D.C.	(4)	139	50.4
Mathematics					
S.C. State*	21	S.C.	(22)	47	44.7
Fayetteville State*	16	N.C.	(38)	58	27.6
Morgan State*	13	Md.	(19)	39	33.3
Univ. of D.C.*	11	D.C.	(7)	19	57.9
Bowie State*	11	Md.	(19)	39	28.2
Physical sciences					
Embry-Riddle U.	98	Fla.	(22)	121	81.0
Howard U.*	25	D.C.	(8)	43	58.1
Xavier U.*	16	La.	(18)	43	37.2
Univ. of D.C.*	15	D.C.	(8)	43	34.9
Alcorn State*	13^d	Miss.	(14)	48	27.1
Hampton U.*	13^d	Va.	(30)	37	35.1
Fisk U.*	13^d	Tenn.	(30)	38	34.2

NOTES: The top five institutions and their percent contribution to their states, 1980–1981.

[a]$N1$ = number of degrees awarded by a given institution; $N2$ = number of degrees awarded in a given state.

[b]The range for the number of baccalaureate degrees awarded to blacks in the biological sciences by a single institution was 0–78; in engineering, 0–153; in mathematics, 0–21; in the physical sciences, 0–98.

[c]The numbers in parentheses represent the total number of reporting institutions in a given state.

[d]These three institutions awarded the same number of B.A. degrees to blacks in the physical sciences; therefore they were tied for fifth place.

*Predominantly black colleges and universities.

TABLE 3.5   Masters' Degrees Awarded to Blacks

Institution	$N1^a$	State		$N2^a$	Percent
Biological sciences					
Atlanta U.*	11^b	Ga.	$(12)^c$	13	84.6
Howard U.*	9	D.C.	(6)	10	90.0
Alabama State*	7	Al.	(12)	13	53.8
Grambling State*	6	La.	(10)	8	75.0
Engineering					
Polytechnic Inst.					
of New York	27	N.Y.	(18)	62	43.5
CUNY-City	12	N.Y.	(18)	62	19.4
Cornell U.	11	N.Y.	(18)	62	17.7
Howard U.*	11	D.C.	(3)	23	47.8
Mathematics					
Southern U.*	5	La.	(9)	7	71.4
Atlanta U.*	4	Ga.	(6)	7	57.0
Rochester Tech.	3^d	N.Y.	(36)	14	21.4
Prairie View*	3^d	Tex.	(25)	6	50.0
N.C. A & T.*	3^d	N.C.	(9)	3	100.0
Texas Southern*	3^d	Tex.	(25)	6	50.0
Physical sciences					
Atlanta U.*	14	Ga.	(8)	18	77.8
Howard U.*	7	D.C.	(5)	10	70.0
Jackson State*	6	Miss.	(4)	8	75.0
Prairie View*	4	Tex.	(28)	8	50.0

NOTES: The top five institutions and their percent contribution to their states, 1980–1981.

[a]$N1$ = number of degrees awarded by a given institution; $N2$ = number of degrees awarded in a given state.

[b]The range for the number of masters' degrees awarded to blacks in the biological sciences by a single institution was 0–11; in engineering, 0–27; in mathematics, 0–5; in the physical sciences, 0–14.

[c]The numbers in parentheses represent the total number of reporting institutions in a given state.

[d]These four institutions awarded the same number of B.A. degrees to blacks in the physical sciences; therefore they were tied for fifth place.

*Predominantly black colleges and universities.

TABLE 3.6   Doctors' Degrees Awarded to Blacks

Institution	$N1^a$	State		$N2^a$	Percent
Biological sciences					
Atlanta U.*	9^b	Ga.	$(4)^c$	11	81.8
Howard U.*	10	D.C.	(4)	11	90.9
Engineering					
Cornell U.	5	N.Y.	(13)	7	71.4
Univ. of Mass.–Amherst	3	Mass.	(6)	3	100.0
Mathematics^d					
—	—	—	—	—	—
Physical sciences					
Univ. of Illinois–					
Urbana	4	Ill.	(8)	5	80.0
Howard U.*	4	D.C.	(5)	6	66.7

NOTES: The top five institutions and their percent contribution to their states, 1980–1981.
^{a}$N1$ = number of degrees awarded by a given institution; $N2$ = number of degrees awarded in a given state.
^{b}The range for the number of doctoral degrees awarded to blacks in the biological sciences by a single institution was 0–10; in engineering, 0–5; in the physical sciences, 0–4.
^{c}The numbers in parentheses represent the total number of reporting institutions in a given state.
^{d}At the Ph.D. level there were no major producers in mathematics.
*Predominantly black colleges and universities.

Carolina A. and T. State University, Prairie View A. and M. University, and the University of the District of Columbia in engineering; the University of the District of Columbia in mathematics; and Embry-Riddle and Howard University in physical sciences. These institutions made a 50 percent or greater contribution to their state's production of black bachelor's degree recipients in the four fields shown in Table 3.4. (Howard University and the University of the District of Columbia are located in Washington).

The top four institutions in awarding masters' degrees to blacks in the natural and technical sciences are reported in Table 3.5. Again, the TBIs took the lead. In fact, in the biological and physical sciences, all of the leading institutions are TBIs; in mathematics, all but one (Rochester Technical Institute) of the leading institutions are TBIs. These institutions also made a substantial contribution at the master's degree level to their state's production of black degree recipients in the natural and technical sciences in 1980/1981. This was especially true in the biological and physical sciences where 50 percent or more of the black masters' recipients were produced by these institutions.

In engineering, Table 3.5 shows that the majority of the leading institutions (three out of four) that awarded masters' degrees to blacks in 1980/1981 were predominantly white institutions rather than TBIs. These were the Polytechnic Institute of New York, CUNY–City College, and Cornell University. Howard University, a TBI, tied for third with Cornell. Also, Howard and the Polytechnic Institute of New York contributed over 40 percent to their states' pool of black master's degree recipients in engineering.

Table 3.6 shows the top two institutions in awarding Ph.D. degrees to blacks in the biological sciences, engineering, and the physical sciences. Because there were very few institutions awarding doctoral degrees to blacks in the natural and technical sciences and very few blacks who earned degrees in these fields, two was the highest number of institutions that could appropriately be designated at the doctoral level. Note the range for the number of degrees awarded to blacks by institutions at this level. There were no leading institutions in the production of black Ph.D.s in mathematics in 1980/1981. A total of nine doctoral degrees were awarded to blacks in mathematics in that year. One degree was awarded by each of these institutions.

Table 3.6 shows that four was the maximum number of doctoral degrees awarded to blacks in 1980/1981 by any single institution in the physical sciences; a total of five in engineering and a total of ten in the biological sciences. Both of the two leading institutions that produced black Ph.D.s in the biological sciences were TBIs (Howard University and Atlanta University). These institutions comprised from 82 to 91 percent of their states' total production of black doctoral recipients in the biological sciences. Howard University was also one of the two leading institutions (along with the University of Illinois–Urbana) that awarded doctoral degrees in the physical sciences to blacks. However none of the TBIs offered doctoral degrees in engineering; therefore, two PWIs (Cornell University and the University of Massachusetts–Amherst) produced a total of eight black doctorates in engineering in 1980/1981. These two institutions, as well as the two leading institutions in the physical sciences and the biological sciences, made a 67 to 100 percent contribution to the total of doctoral degrees in the natural and technical sciences awarded to blacks in their states.

To summarize, the findings revealed that despite desegregation in higher education and increased educational opportunity for blacks in the 1970s, black students remained severely underrepresented in the natural and technical sciences in U.S. colleges and universities in the 1980s. Black students were most severely underrepresented in the natural and technical sciences at the graduate level; however, even at the undergraduate level—especially in engineering and the physical sciences—they were underrepresented relative to their availability among black college students in general and relative to their representation in the U.S. college-aged population. The data also showed that although black males generally exceeded black females in enrollment and degree attainment in the natural and technical sciences, the disparity favoring black males was primarily at the graduate rather than at the undergraduate level. In addition, sex disparities in enrollment and degree attainment favoring males in the natural and technical sciences were greater among white students than among black students at both the undergraduate and graduate levels.

An assessment of the progress of U.S. colleges and universities showed that while the nation's PWIs were the prime producers of the limited pool of black doctoral recipients in the natural and technical sciences, the TBIs were the major granters of degrees to blacks at the master's and baccalaureate levels. More specifically, the TBIs were among the top four or five institutions in the production of black baccalaureate and master's degree recipients in the natural and technical sciences. Previous studies by Jay (1971) and Pearson and Pearson (1985) indicated that the traditionally black institutions were the primary educators of black scientists and black students in general prior to desegregation of higher education. The findings in this study illustrate that even after desegregation of higher education and the subsequent decline in black student enrollment at black colleges, these institutions continue to be the prime producers of the nation's black students for graduate education.

This chapter clearly highlights two important realities. The first is that black students are still primarily outsiders with reference to natural and technical science majors and careers. Studies have indicated that these fields, along with the traditional professions (law, medicine, and so on), are among the nation's most lucrative careers (Goldman and Hewitt 1976; Sells 1976). In addition, race and sex disparities in income and occupational attainment have been attributed partly to the lower representation of blacks and women in scientific and technical fields and their overrepresentation in education, the social sciences, and other less lucrative fields. Thus, greater and more effective efforts must be employed to increase the educational and occupational attainment of blacks and other minorities in the natural and technical sciences.

Such efforts should entail increasing financial aid (especially grant aid) and mentor-protégé opportunities in mathematics and science for black students, or alternatively, awarding more money and prestige to individuals who are pursuing careers in the humanities, social sciences, and arts. In addition, efforts to improve the standardized test performance of blacks through pre-college preparation in test-taking skills and to improve the analytical and academic ability of black students in general should be useful. Alternatives to traditional methods of identifying, recruiting, and nurturing minority talent are needed. One method might be to rely more on academic grades than on standardized test performance in evaluating the academic ability and potential of black students. A second strategy would be to rely on individuals in the local community of minority students to identify minority talent.

Improving the elementary and secondary education of minority students and implementing student and institutional intervention strategies at the elementary and junior high school levels are also critical needs. Most students have formulated their educational and career aspirations as early as ninth grade and are academically tracked for future college and vocational education and careers by this time (McBay 1984; Parsons 1959; Sells 1976). Thus early rather than late (i.e., before high school) educational intervention to prepare black students for future mathematics and science education and careers is extremely important.

The second striking reality revealed by the findings in this chapter concerns the role of the nation's TBIs. The data clearly illustrate the important role that these institutions continue to play in educating black students. It is predicted that TBIs will be required to assume an even greater responsibility in educating black students as tuition and academic standards for admissions continue to escalate at the PWIs (Copeland 1984; Council of Graduate Schools in the U.S. 1984). However, inadequate finances and academic resources continue to constitute prime problems at both public and private black colleges (Scott 1981; Garibaldi 1984). Greater efforts to support these institutions and to strengthen and develop further programs in the natural and technical sciences are needed to assure their survival and future success in educating black students. In addition, PWIs may require greater financial and other incentives to increase their ability to recruit and retain black students in the natural and technical sciences. The identification and findings regarding black and white institutions that were leaders in the production of black degree recipients also suggest the need for follow-up studies to determine what factors contribute to the success of these institutions.

Finally, greater moral and social support as well as financial commitment must be demonstrated by the federal and state governments and by college, university, and elementary and secondary school administrators to facilitate the access and success of black students in the natural and technical sciences. At the same time, black students and their parents must not rely primarily on government and educational initiatives to do the job for them. They must take the lead in preparing black students to pursue successfully careers in mathematics and science. This should include becoming more knowledgeable about tracking practices in public schools and about educational requirements and opportunities for minorities in mathematics and science.

Black students and the black community must also increase their awareness of the importance of mathematics and science, and must develop formal and informal networks to encourage, motivate, and facilitate the interest, access, and achievement of blacks in these fields. However, these and other efforts by blacks are not enough; they must be part of a broader plan of implementation that is established and supported by the total society. This is essential because the underrepresentation of blacks and other minorities in the natural and technical sciences translates as America's underrepresentation worldwide. Thus the problem must be addressed as a societal problem rather than a black problem if America expects to actualize fully the mathematics and science potential of all youth and maintain its global position of achievement and respect in science and technology.

4

A Statistical Portrait
of Black Ph.D.s

The black research scholar may be a rare and vanishing breed, particularly in such disciplines as mathematics, the physical sciences, and engineering (Staples 1986). Given projected demographic trends, concern is being expressed about the nation's ability to maintain its scientific and technical human-resource base over the next decade or two. A frequently advocated strategy for addressing this concern is to increase recruiting from such groups as women and members of racial and ethnic minority populations that have traditionally been underrepresented in these disciplines (Office of Technological Assessment 1985).

This study examines one particular group—blacks with doctorates in science and engineering fields—and generates a statistical portrait of their career participation and development in these fields. The study is based on data generated by two surveys of the doctorate population: 1) the Survey of Doctorate Recipients—a biennial longitudinal survey of a sample of doctorate holders; and 2) the Survey of Earned Doctorates—an annual survey of new doctoral degree recipients. The analysis covers the 1975–1985 period and includes information describing behavioral and social scientists as well as natural scientists and engineers. For the most part, the study confines itself to American citizens; foreign citizens are excluded. Finally, wherever possible, the analysis highlights differences between blacks and comparable whites.

Blacks in the Ph.D. Population

The number of blacks with Ph.D.s in science and engineering fields more than doubled in the last ten years. Although the trend patterns are roughly similar for blacks and whites, the rate of increase is slightly larger for blacks. Thus, the percentage of all Ph.D.s who are black has been rising slowly—from 1.0 in 1975 to 1.3 in 1985. In contrast, blacks constitute about 11 percent of the 1985 civilian noninstitutional population, sixteen years old and above, 6 percent of all those employed in 1984 in professional specialties, and 2 percent of employed scientists and engineers at all degree levels (National Science Foundation 1986; U.S. Bureau of the Census 1985). An implication of this disproportionately low number of black Ph.D.s is that there are factors operating in our society that increase barriers to (or reduce incentives for) their pursuit of careers at the graduate level in science or engineering.

When the data are separated into broad fields, it is found that the rising trend in the black share of the doctorate population over the 1975–1985 period is attributable solely to increasing shares in social sciences and psychology (Table 4.1). Although the number of black Ph.D.s increased dramatically in the life sciences and in the broad field that includes mathematics, computer sciences, and engineering, little or no change occurred in the black shares of the populations in these fields. Both the number and proportion of blacks in physical science fields fell.

Over four-fifths of the black Ph.D.s are clustered in psychology, social sciences, and life sciences (Figure 4.1). When standardized for field size, however, concentration is most pronounced in the former two fields (Table 4.1). There are relatively few black Ph.D.s in the broad field that includes mathematics, computer sciences, and engineering (hereafter referred to as MCSE fields), and in the physical sciences.

Black females have entered the science and engineering doctorate population more successfully than have black males (Table 4.2). Black females constitute 2.9 percent of the 1985 female science and engineering doctorate

TABLE 4.1   Black Ph.D.s by Broad Field

	1985		1981		1975	
Field	N	%	N	%	N	%
Physical sciences	467	0.5	573	0.7	538	0.8
Mathematics, computer sciences, engineering	414	0.5	391	0.6	218	0.4
Life sciences	1,287	1.2	989	1.1	844	1.3
Psychology	1,186	2.1	800	1.8	359	1.3
Social sciences	1,610	2.8	949	2.0	448	1.3
All fields	4,964	1.3	3,702	1.1	2,407	1.0

SOURCE: Unpublished tabulations, National Research Council.
NOTE: Total population and as a percent of all Ph.D.s, 1975–1985.

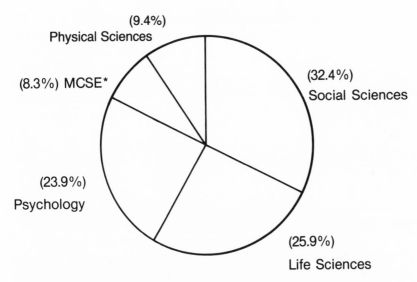

(9.4%) Physical Sciences

(8.3%) MCSE*

(32.4%) Social Sciences

(23.9%) Psychology

(25.9%) Life Sciences

FIGURE 4.1   Distribution of Black Ph.D.s (by Broad Field of Science, 1985)

population. The comparable figure for black males is only one percent. Despite a greater tendency for black females to cluster in life, social, and behavioral sciences (over 90 percent for females versus about 75 percent for males), higher entry rates (i.e., black females as a percentage of all female doctorates) are evident in each major field.

An important factor underlying the relatively low representation of blacks among Ph.D.s in science and engineering fields is the relatively high rate of attrition of blacks from the educational pipeline. Astin (1982) presents evidence in support of this conclusion in his study. He concludes that black underrepresentation appears to be attributable to greater-than-white losses from the educational pipeline at all transition points.

In her comprehensive study of women and minorities in quantitative fields, Berryman (1983, 5) concludes that field choices of blacks who remain in the pipeline are also important determinants of underrepresentation.

When we examine field choices, we find that field choices also contribute to blacks' underrepresentation among quantitative B.A., M.A., and Ph.D. degrees. Blacks lose "field" ground just as they lose attainment ground: at several points in the process. At the B.A. level, the percent choosing quantitative fields is 60 percent of the national average; at the M.A. level, 40 percent; and at the Ph.D. level, 33 percent.

TABLE 4.2   Black Ph.D.s by Broad Field and Sex

	Males		Females	
Field	N	%	N	%
Physical sciences	396	0.5	71	1.2
Mathematics, computer sciences, engineering	375	0.5	39	1.4
Life sciences	790	0.9	497	2.5
Psychology	569	1.5	617	3.5
Social sciences	1,178	2.6	432	3.9
All fields	3,308	1.0	1,656	2.9

SOURCE: Unpublished tabulations, National Research Council.
NOTE: Total population and as a percent of all Ph.D.s, 1985.

In part, the origins of these observed differences lie in black/white disparities in course-taking behavior, particularly during the precollege years. Although there is no strong evidence indicating that black high school students take fewer years of math and science than white students, a smaller proportion of black high school students take the advanced courses—especially in math, physics, and chemistry, as is shown by Josephine D. Davis and Bernice Anderson in this volume.

Ph.D. Attainment

The annual number of new black Ph.D.s in science and engineering increased from 261 in 1975 to 293 in 1985—an average increase of 1.2 percent per year. Although the trend continues to be positive, the rate has declined dramatically over this period—from 1.5 percent per year between 1975 and 1980 to 0.8 percent per year between 1980 and 1985. Over this same 1975–1985 period, the total number of new Ph.D.s produced annually in science and engineering fields declined by almost 10 percent, resulting in an increase in the black share of new Ph.D.s awarded in these fields from 1.8 percent in 1975 to 2.2 percent in 1985. Given the patterns of attrition outlined above, there is little expectation that this share will rise dramatically in the near future.

The tendency of black Ph.D. holders to cluster in psychology and social and life sciences is also found among new Ph.D. recipients. Over 80 percent of the new black Ph.D. recipients were found in those fields; none of the remaining fields awarded more than twenty degrees to blacks in any of the years reported (Figure 4.2).

Blacks are older than whites at the time they receive their degrees. In part, this is due to blacks' clustering in fields in which the age at degree completion is higher than the average. In 1985, for example, the median age of blacks receiving degrees in psychology and social sciences was 33.9 years and for whites it was 32.9 years compared to medians in all fields of 33.2 and 30.9, respectively. An additional reason, however, is that blacks take longer to complete their Ph.D. training. The median time from the receipt of the baccalaureate to the receipt of the Ph.D. was 10.3 for blacks and 8.2 for whites in 1985. These medians have been rising between 1975 and 1985 for both blacks and whites—reflecting, perhaps, the poor state of employment opportunities in most fields during this period. The largest number of years between baccalaureate and Ph.D. for blacks is partially due to the greater amount of time blacks spend in nonregistered status, almost twice as much as do whites—2.8 years versus 1.5 years.

A possible factor explaining the black/white difference in time required to complete the Ph.D. is sources of funding for graduate training, which have shifted dramatically for both blacks and whites between 1975 and 1985 (Table 4.3).

A smaller fraction of these degree recipients report the federal government as a major source of support, and the decline was larger for whites than for blacks. Offsetting the loss of funding support, a larger fraction report loans, own (or family) sources, or "other" sources (mainly funding from state and local government or university sources).

Loans appear to be the major source of funds used to offset the decreasing importance of federal support. These now outweigh federal sources in impor-

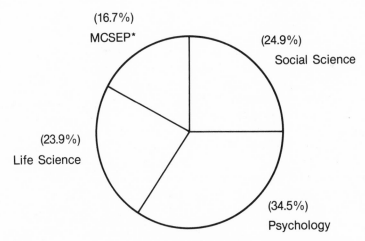

FIGURE 4.2   Percentage Distribution of Newly Awarded Black Ph.D.s (by Broad Field of Science, 1985)

TABLE 4.3   Sources of Support for Ph.D. Training

Type of support	1975	1980	1985
Federal support			
Black	55.2%	40.6%	38.6%
White	57.1	36.5	24.8
Loan support			
Black	29.1	35.9	43.7
White	17.3	18.3	35.1
Own support			
Black	63.6	58.0	72.4
White	64.6	63.7	76.9
"Other" support			
Black	77.4	72.6	78.8
White	88.3	81.9	86.8

SOURCE: Unpublished tabulations, National Research Council.
NOTE: For blacks and whites, 1975–1985.

tance for both blacks and whites. "Other" sources of support continue to be the dominant funding source for both races. These findings about funding sources apply equally to each of the major fields of science and engineering, with the notable exception of the life sciences, in which the federal government has maintained its relative importance as a funding source.

Transition to Work

Employment opportunities for blacks—measured in terms of the percentage who had definite employment plans at the time they received their degrees—have deteriorated between 1975 and 1985 relative to those for whites. In 1975, regardless of race, roughly one out of every four respondents indicated that they had no definite employment plans (Table 4.4). By 1985 the rate for blacks increased to two out of five respondents, while the rate remained essentially unchanged at 1985 levels for whites. As a result, in 1985 the percentage with no definite plans at the time of graduation was half again as high for blacks as it was for whites (39 percent versus 26 percent). The deterioration in employment opportunities for blacks suggested by this indicator was most pronounced in the social sciences, where the percentage with no definite plans almost doubled between 1975 and 1985 (from 23 percent to 42 percent).

Of those who report definite plans, the percentage anticipating academic employment dropped dramatically between 1975 and 1985 for both blacks and whites (Table 4.4). The decline for blacks was larger than the decline for whites. Thus, the differential in academic employment opportunities that favored blacks in 1975 has narrowed considerably from 23 percentage points in 1975 to 11 percentage points in 1985. Field-specific trends reinforce commonly held views about the field variability in academic employment conditions. For both blacks and whites, the decline was most dramatic in the social sciences; for whites with degrees in engineering, the academic share has hovered around 25 percent over the past ten years.

Unemployment and Underemployment

Since practically all Ph.D.s who are willing to work are employed, an assessment of the efficiency with which they are utilized must be based on more than just unemployment. This study uses an indicator that adds underemployment (those who are employed part time but seeking full-time work and those who

TABLE 4.4   Postgraduate Plans of New Ph.D.s

| | Percent with no definite plans | | | | | |
| | 1975 | | 1980 | | 1985 | |
Field	Black	White	Black	White	Black	White
All fields	24.1	24.0	28.1	22.5	38.6	25.8
Physical sciences						
& mathematics	29.3	24.9	24.0	18.0	43.3	21.5
Engineering	18.2	20.5	18.2	15.1	36.8	19.9
Life sciences	23.2	22.8	21.5	22.3	28.6	25.4
Social sciences &						
psychology	23.5	25.5	31.7	27.4	42.0	30.7

	Percent with postgraduate plans for academic employment					
All fields	61.1	38.3	51.0	30.4	38.3	27.0
Physical sciences						
& mathematics	41.4	26.1	31.6	22.6	29.4	20.3
Engineering	33.3	25.4	44.4	25.2	16.7	25.0
Life sciences	48.8	29.4	45.1	23.7	42.0	22.2
Social sciences &						
psychology	72.6	58.8	56.9	43.8	40.6	38.1

SOURCE: Unpublished tabulations, National Research Council.
NOTE: For blacks and whites, by broad field: 1975, 1980, 1985.

TABLE 4.5   Underutilization Rates for Ph.D.s

Field	Total Black	Total White	Male Black	Male White	Female Black	Female White
All fields	3.7	2.0	3.8	1.5	3.7	4.7
Physical sciences	0.9	1.3	0.5	1.1	2.9	4.3
Mathematics, computer sciences & engineering	1.7	1.2	1.9	1.1	?	1.9
Life sciences	3.1	2.2	1.8	1.6	5.1	4.6
Psychology	2.9	2.4	3.0	1.9	2.8	3.4
Social sciences	6.3	3.5	7.1	2.5	4.1	7.9

SOURCE: Unpublished tabulations, National Research Council.
NOTE: As percent of total work force, for blacks and whites, by broad field and sex, 1985.

TABLE 4.6   Underutilization Rates of Ph.D.s in the Total Work Force

	1985 Black	1985 White	1981 Black	1981 White	1975 Black	1975 White
Total underutilization	3.7	2.0	2.7	1.6	1.5	1.9
Unemployed	1.4	0.8	1.8	0.7	1.1	0.9
Employed part-time, seeking full-time	1.2	0.7	0.4	0.6	0	0.7
Involuntarily in non-science and engineering	1.1	0.4	0.5	0.3	0.4	0.3

SOURCE: Unpublished tabulations, National Research Council.
NOTE: By race and type of underutilization: 1975, 1981, 1985.

are involuntarily employed outside of science and engineering fields) to the traditional indicator—unemployment—to derive a measure of *underutilization*. When compared to aggregate measures of unemployment, the 1985 underutilization rates for Ph.D. scientists and engineers is quite low—2.5 percent, compared with an underutilization rate of 4.1 percent for all scientists and engineers and an unemployment rate in excess of 7 percent for the entire labor force. The underutilization rate for black Ph.D.s, however, is higher than the rate for whites, 3.7 percent versus 2.0 percent (Table 4.5).

In part, the observed black/white differential can be attributed to differences in field distribution. Blacks are more heavily concentrated in the social sciences, a broad field for which the underutilization rates are considerably higher than average, regardless of race or sex. When weighted by the field distribution of the Ph.D. population the average black/white difference in underutilization narrows substantially—from 1.7 percentage points to 0.5 percentage points.

Table 4.5 also reveals the striking finding of a strong race-sex interaction with respect to underutilization rates. Although black men have higher rates of underutilization than white men, the black/white differential is reversed for women. Black females have rates that are over 20 percent lower than those of white women. Moreover, with the exception of the life sciences, the direction of the black/white differential continues to favor black women even when the data are further separated by broad fields.

Since 1975 underutilization rates have been rising dramatically for black Ph.D.s, while for white Ph.D.s they have been displaying virtually no trend (Table 4.6). The major reason for the observed increase in the black/white differential has been the increases for blacks in underemployment (involuntary employment in part-time jobs or in nonscience or nonengineering activity). This finding underscores the significance of using a concept of utilization for Ph.D.s that goes beyond simply whether they are unemployed. Failure to have considered the aspects of underemployment summarized in Figure 4.3 would have resulted in an understatement of the relative deterioration that has occurred for black Ph.D.s in their utilization rates.

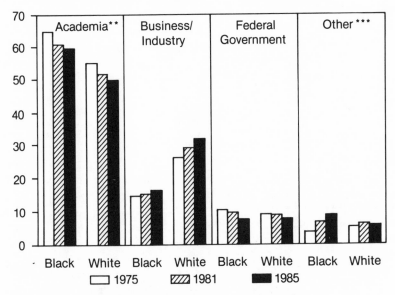

FIGURE 4.3   Employment Trends by Selected Sectors (for Black and White Ph.D.s, 1975–1985)

TABLE 4.7   Ph.D.s by Field and Sector of Employment

Sector of employment	All fields		Physical sciences		MCSE[a] fields		Life sciences		Psychology		Social sciences	
	B	W	B	W	B	W	B	W	B	W	B	W
Total employed	100.0	100.0	100.0	100.0	100.0	100.0	100.0	100.0	100.0	100.0	100.0	100.0
Educational Institutions												
Four-year colleges/ universities/medical schools	63.7	52.2	47.4	39.9	51.5	47.1	63.8	60.6	55.8	45.3	79.9	70.5
	59.9	49.8	47.0	38.1	50.7	46.3	59.8	58.5	47.1	39.6	76.0	68.2
Business/industry	16.3	31.8	34.5	46.3	38.1	43.4	10.8	21.3	17.4	31.1	8.2	13.3
U.S. government	7.3	7.5	17.7	8.9	10.0	6.8	11.8	9.3	2.0	3.2	4.3	7.5
State/local government	5.2	2.0	0.0	1.1	0.0	0.3	7.6	2.3	7.8	4.1	4.4	3.2
Hospitals/clinics	3.9	3.0	0.4	0.6	0.0	0.1	4.5	3.2	11.0	11.1	0.2	1.2
Other/nonprofit organizations	3.5	3.4	0.0	3.3	0.5	2.2	1.5	3.3	6.1	4.2	5.0	4.4

SOURCE: Unpublished tabulations, National Research Council.
NOTES: Percent of blacks and whites, 1985.
[a]Mathematics, computer sciences, and engineering.

Employment Sectors

The academic and business sectors of the economy provided more than three-quarters of the 1985 employment of black and white Ph.D.s. Regardless of race, the most important employer of Ph.D.s in our economy is the academic sector—in particular, four-year colleges, universities, and medical schools, which in 1985 employed almost three out of every five black Ph.D.s and almost one out of two white Ph.D.s (Table 4.7).

There is a considerable amount of field variation in the relative importance of academia as a source of employment for Ph.D.s. Those with Ph.D.s in the social sciences are most heavily dependent regardless of race. More than two-thirds of white social scientists and over three-fourths of the black social scientists had academic jobs. Ph.D.s in the physical sciences and in psychology are least dependent on academia as a source of employment. Less than two-fifths of the employed white Ph.D.s in these fields and less than one-half of the employed black Ph.D.s in these fields had academic jobs.

Industry is the next most important employer of Ph.D.s regardless of race. Unlike in academia, however, white Ph.D.s were twice as likely to be employed in the sector as black Ph.D.s (32 percent versus 16 percent). Part of the black/white differential in industrial employment can be attributed to differences in field distributions. As noted earlier, blacks are more heavily concentrated in the social, behavioral, and life sciences—broad fields for which industry is a relatively less important source of employment. When weighted by field distribution of the Ph.D. population (total for all races), the average black/white difference narrows from 16 percentage points to 10 percentage points.

The federal government is the third most important employer of Ph.D.s. The black/white differential in this sector has a strong field interaction. It is a more important source of employment for blacks in the physical sciences, MCSE fields, and in the life sciences. It is a less important source of employment for blacks relative to whites in the fields of psychology and social sciences.

Table 4.7 also reveals the importance of hospitals and clinics as a source of employment for Ph.D.s in psychology. Although only 3 percent of the white Ph.D.s and 4 percent of the black Ph.D.s in all fields are employed in this sector, it accounts for over 12 percent of the employed white psychologists and 11 percent of the black psychologists.

The sectoral distribution of employment shifts dramatically from 1975 to 1985 for both black and white Ph.D.s (Figure 4.3). Academia declines in importance for both. For blacks, academia's share of employment declines from 65 to 60 percent; for whites, the decline is from 55 to 50 percent. The federal government also declines in relative importance for both blacks and whites, dropping from 10 percent in 1975 to about 7 percent in 1985.

Offsetting these declining trends in academia and the federal government, the role of industry as an employer of Ph.D.s expands dramatically. Figure 4.3 shows that the increase for white Ph.D.s is larger than the increase for black Ph.D.s. The origin of this growing black/white differential is in the physical sciences—a broad field in which the black share of industrial employment falls from 38 percent in 1975 to 34 percent in 1985.

State and local governments and nonprofit organizations also become increasingly important as employers of black Ph.D.s, more than doubling their share of black employment over this period (from roughly 3.5 percent in 1975 to almost 9 percent in 1985).

Primary Work Activity

The findings with respect to work activity (i.e., the activity identified by the survey respondents as their "primary activity") reflect earlier findings on sector of employment. Those who report working in academia are more likely to report teaching or research and development as their major work activity. Similarly, those who report industry as their sector of employment are more likely to report either research and development or management as their primary work activity.

Recall that blacks are more likely to report academia as their sector of employment than comparable whites. Accordingly, it is not surprising that the most important activity reported by blacks in 1985 is teaching. Almost two out of five black Ph.D.s indicate teaching as their major work activity. Similarly, since white Ph.D.s are more likely to report industry as their employment sector than comparable blacks, it is not surprising that almost one-third of the white Ph.D.s indicate that research and development was their major work activity (Table 4.8).

These findings, however, are subject to strong field interactions. For example, although teaching is the most important activity reported by black Ph.D.s combined over all fields, research and development is the most important activity reported by blacks in physical science (42 percent) and in MCSE fields (35 percent). Similarly, although research and development is the most important activity reported by white Ph.D.s, teaching is the most important occupation reported by white Ph.D.s in the social sciences (52 percent). Regardless of race, Ph.D.s in psychology report consulting as their most important activity (42 percent for blacks and 44 percent for whites).

A larger share of black Ph.D.s report management or administration as their work activity than comparable whites (24 percent versus 19 percent). This finding suggests that although blacks may have less representation in business and industry than comparable whites, they may be moving up the

TABLE 4.8 Science Ph.D.s by Field and Primary Work Activity

Primary Work Activity	All fields		Physical sciences		MCSE[a] fields		Life sciences		Psychology		Social sciences	
	B	W	B	W	B	W	B	W	B	W	B	W
Total employed	100.0	100.0	100.0	100.0	100.0	100.0	100.0	100.0	100.0	100.0	100.0	100.0
Teaching	38.4	28.9	24.5	21.7	34.2	29.0	33.4	24.9	26.2	24.0	57.3	52.4
Management/ administration	23.8	18.8	27.5	21.6	22.2	23.4	29.3	17.5	18.9	13.0	22.7	16.7
Research & development	16.5	31.9	37.7	41.9	36.7	34.5	20.5	40.9	8.9	13.2	7.1	16.6
Consulting/ professional services	14.6	12.5	5.2	5.1	1.5	6.7	9.1	8.5	41.9	44.1	4.3	6.4
Writing/editing	2.7	2.3	2.5	2.3	2.9	1.1	2.5	2.3	0.8	2.5	4.4	3.7
Other activity	3.9	5.5	2.5	7.5	2.4	5.3	5.2	5.9	3.3	3.2	4.3	4.3

SOURCE: Unpublished tabulations, National Research Council.
NOTES: Percent of blacks and whites, 1985.
[a]Mathematics, computer sciences, and engineering.

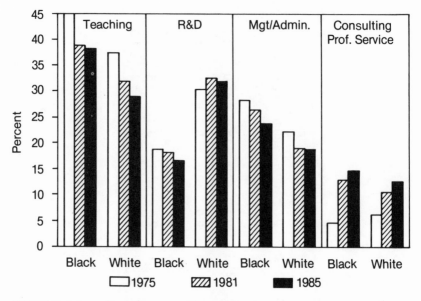

FIGURE 4.4   Employment Trends by Selected Work Activities (for Black and White Ph.D.s, 1975–1985)

career ladder at a more rapid rate. Alternatively, it is possible that these findings reflect a larger fraction of academically employed black Ph.D.s in management or administrative positions. Except for MCSE fields—where the fraction of Ph.D.s reporting management and administration is essentially equal for blacks and whites—a greater proportion of black Ph.D.s are employed in managerial or administrative activities in all major fields.

Figure 4.4 summarizes trends in work activities for the period 1975 through 1985. As was true for employment sector, significant shifts in work activities for both black and white Ph.D.s are revealed. The relative importance of teaching and management or administrative activities has declined for both black and white Ph.D.s over this period.

These declines are offset by the increasing importance of consulting and professional services. The proportion of black Ph.D.s reporting these activities more than tripled over this period, while the proportion of white Ph.D.s reporting these activities almost doubled. The rapid and dramatic increase in the importance of consulting and professional services as an activity for Ph.D.s can be attributed largely to the substantial increase in the proportion of psychologists of both races who report these activities. For black Ph.D.s, this proportion increased from 15 percent in 1975 to 42 percent in 1985; for white Ph.D.s, this proportion increased from 29 percent in 1975 to 44 percent in 1985.

The proportion of Ph.D.s reporting research and development as their major activity remained reasonably stable over this period. It increased slightly for white Ph.D.s and decreased slightly for black Ph.D.s.

Tenure Status

The proportion of employed Ph.D.s who are tenured is a commonly accepted measure of career advancement in academia. In 1985 almost two-thirds of the white Ph.D.s and roughly three out of five black Ph.D.s reported that they had tenure (Table 4.9). The black/white differential in tenure status varied significantly by field both in direction and magnitude. Blacks are likely to be tenured in the fields of physical science (where 41 percent had tenure compared with 70 percent of white Ph.D.s) and in psychology (where 44 percent of the black Ph.D.s had tenure compared with 60 percent of the white Ph.D.s). White Ph.D.s are more likely to be tenured in MCSE fields (81 percent versus 72 percent for black Ph.D.s). Black and white Ph.D.s are equally likely to be tenured in the fields of the life and social sciences.

Table 4.9 also summarizes differences in tenure status by race and sex for both black and white Ph.D.s. It shows that black females are less likely to be tenured than black males (47 percent versus 67 percent) but are more likely to be tenured than white females (47 percent versus 44 percent). Separation by field does not alter the former conclusion, but it does reveal exceptions to the latter conclusion in the fields of psychology and the social sciences. Table 4.9 also reveals that the main difference in tenure status between black females and white males arises solely from the effects of gender on tenure status. Except for the fields of psychology and the social sciences, the race effect favors black females.

Regardless of race, the proportion of academically employed Ph.D.s with tenure increased between 1975 and 1985. This increasing trend—which reflects the dramatic buildup in academic employment that occurred in the 1960s—is found for both blacks and whites of both genders and, with the exception of physical science and psychology, is experienced in all fields.

Academic Rank

Most academically employed Ph.D.s are faculty members. Table 4.10 reveals that over 85 percent of the academically employed black and white Ph.D.s are members of faculties. The results vary, however, by field. Black Ph.D.s in the physical sciences are less likely to be faculty members than comparable white Ph.D.s (66 percent versus 82 percent).

TABLE 4.9   Academically Employed, Tenured Ph.D.s

Total academic employment	All fields		Physical sciences		MCSE[a] fields		Life sciences		Psychology		Social sciences	
	B	W	B	W	B	W	B	W	B	W	B	W
Total tenured	61.1	66.6	41.2	69.5	81.0	72.4	62.9	62.5	44.0	60.8	67.8	68.8
Male tenured	67.0	70.6	39.6	71.1	81.3	73.6	67.7	67.8	48.2	68.2	75.2	73.0
Female tenured	47.2	43.6	55.6	45.8	77.8	49.9	56.4	37.8	38.8	42.3	41.5	50.9

SOURCE: Unpublished tabulations, National Research Council.
NOTES: Percent of blacks and whites, by field of Ph.D. and sex, 1985.
[a] Mathematics, computer sciences, and engineering.

TABLE 4.10   Faculty Ph.D.s by Field

Field	Black	White
All fields	86.9	85.9
Physical sciences	66.0	81.5
MCSE^a fields	89.7	92.1
Life sciences	88.9	81.9
Psychology	83.0	84.7
Social sciences	90.6	91.5

SOURCE: Unpublished tabulations, National Research Council.
NOTES: Percent of blacks and whites, 1985.
^{a}Mathematics, computer sciences, and engineering.

Table 4.11 reveals that within faculty ranks, blacks are less likely to be full professors (30 percent versus 46 percent for whites) and are more likely to be associate professors (39 percent versus 28 percent for whites) and assistant professors (23 percent versus 20 percent for whites). The black/white differentials in the likelihood of having attained a given faculty rank continue to apply when the data are separated by broad field.

A notable finding that emerges from the field separation is the unusually low proportion of black Ph.D.s who are full professors in the field of psychology. While almost 30 percent of all black Ph.D.s are full professors, only 16 percent of the black Ph.D.s in psychology have attained this rank. Although a comparable finding holds for white Ph.D.s, the differential is not so dramatic—46 percent for all fields versus 40 percent in psychology.

Table 4.12 summarizes trends in the rank distribution of academically employed Ph.D.s for blacks and whites. It reveals dramatic black/white differences in trends for each rank and a resultant widening of black/white differentials. At the full professor level, the proportion of blacks holding this rank declines from 38 percent in 1975 to 30 percent in 1985, while the proportion of whites at this rank increases from 42 percent to 46 percent over the same period. The result is a quadrupling of the black/white differential from 4 percentage points to 16 percentage points. The major source of decline is in the fields of psychology and the physical sciences. The proportion of black Ph.D.s at the rank of full professor in the field of psychology declines from 35 percent in 1975 to 16 percent in 1985. The proportion of black Ph.D.s in the physical sciences holding this rank declines from 52 percent in 1975 to 42 percent in 1985.

The likelihood of being an associate professor increases for black Ph.D.s (from 31 percent in 1975 to 39 percent in 1985) and declines slightly for white Ph.D.s (from 30 percent in 1975 to 27 percent in 1985). The result of these

TABLE 4.11 Distribution of Ph.D. Faculty (1985)

Total academic employment	All fields		Physical sciences		MCSE[a] fields		Life sciences		Psychology		Social sciences	
	B	W	B	W	B	W	B	W	B	W	B	W
Professor	29.8	45.8	42.3	57.0	43.3	52.0	31.8	41.6	16.5	40.1	30.5	41.5
Associate professor	38.7	27.5	26.1	22.9	35.2	25.7	40.1	27.9	38.1	29.4	40.3	30.8
Assistant professor	23.0	19.6	26.1	14.1	11.0	17.1	21.7	22.1	36.1	22.7	19.8	20.5
Instructor	1.3	1.6	2.8	1.7	0.0	0.6	1.0	2.1	1.8	2.3	1.4	1.3
Other	7.1	5.5	2.8	4.3	10.5	4.5	5.4	6.4	7.5	5.6	8.0	5.8

SOURCE: Unpublished tabulations, National Research Council.
NOTES: Percent of blacks and whites, by field and rank, 1985.
[a]Mathematics, computer sciences, and engineering.

TABLE 4.12   Distribution of Ph.D. Faculty (1975 and 1985)

Rank/Race	1975	1985
Full professor		
Black	38.0	29.8
White	41.7	45.8
Associate professor		
Black	30.7	38.7
White	30.0	27.5
Assistant professor		
Black	24.1	23.0
White	25.7	19.6
Instructor/other		
Black	7.3	8.4
White	2.7	7.1

SOURCE: Unpublished tabulations, National Research Council.
NOTES: Percent of blacks and whites, by rank, 1975 and 1985.

divergent trends is a widening of the black/white differential from virtually zero in 1975 to roughly 11 percentage points favoring blacks in 1985.

At the assistant professor level, the proportion of black Ph.D.s remains relatively stable between 1975 and 1985 at approximately one in four. For white Ph.D.s, this declines steadily from roughly 26 percent in 1975 to 20 percent in 1985. The result of these divergent trends at the assistant professor level is a widening of the black/white differential from virtually zero in 1975 to roughly 3.5 percentage points favoring blacks in 1985.

Salaries

In 1985 black Ph.D.s earned approximately $40,000, up 59 percent from their 1975 levels (Figure 4.5). White Ph.D.s earned roughly $45,000 in 1985, up 73 percent from their 1975 levels. The result of these differential trends has been a widening of the black/white differential in salaries from less than 5 percent in 1975 to approximately 12 percent in 1985. (It should be noted that all of this widening occurred between 1975 and 1981.)

When separated by years of experience, the 1985 differentials narrow. There are virtually no black/white differences for Ph.D.s with less than ten years of experience. For Ph.D.s with more than ten years of experience, there exists a differential of about 5 percent favoring whites.

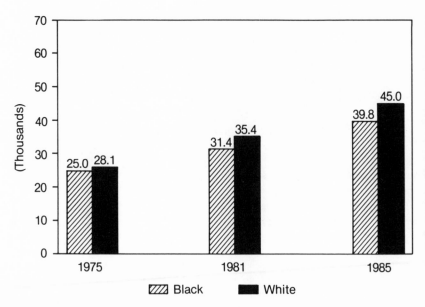

FIGURE 4.5   Median Salaries of Black and White Ph.D.s (in Science and Engineering Fields)

The smaller within-years-of-experience differentials suggest several conclusions. First, a substantial amount of the overall black/white difference in earnings is attributable to differences in age distribution—as much as 80 percent. Second, the larger differential observed at higher years of experience suggests that there may have been unique career-development barriers for older black Ph.D.s. While the absence of black/white differences in earnings for less experienced Ph.D.s is encouraging, it is uncertain that this means eventual elimination of differences for more experienced Ph.D.s in the future.

Figure 4.6 reveals that black/white differences in 1985 salaries are found to be much smaller within major employment sectors than the overall differential averaged over all sectors. The difference for academia and industry was about 7 percent compared with the overall 12 percent difference, and within the federal government the differential was only 2 percent. Unlike in the other major employment sectors, the salaries of black Ph.D.s employed in state and local governments were 13 percent higher than salaries of comparable whites. Among Ph.D.s employed in hospitals and clinics or in other nonprofit institutions, however, the salaries of black Ph.D.s are substantially lower than those of whites (13 percent lower in the former sector and 20 percent lower in the latter).

These findings suggest that a significant amount of the observed differences in salaries between black and white Ph.D.s can be attributed to black/white differences in sectoral distribution in employment. Blacks tend to be more heavily concentrated in educational institutions, where salaries are lower than the average, and whites tend to be more concentrated in business and industry, where salaries tend to be higher than the average.

In summary, a statistical portrait of black Ph.D.s in science and engineering fields has been painted based primarily on data from two major surveys conducted by the National Research Council. Information collected by these surveys permitted an examination of key aspects of their career participation and their career progression.

The data revealed that progress has been slow. The proportion of Ph.D.s who are black has been rising quite slowly—from 1.0 percent in 1975 to only 1.3 percent in 1985. In contrast, blacks constitute 11 percent of the working-aged population (i.e., those who are above the age of fifteen), 6 percent of those employed in professional specialties, and 2 percent of employed scientists and engineers at all degree levels. Moreover, the outlook for improvement in the near term is bleak. The number of new Ph.D.s being awarded to blacks is also rising slowly, and in 1985 the 293 degrees awarded in science

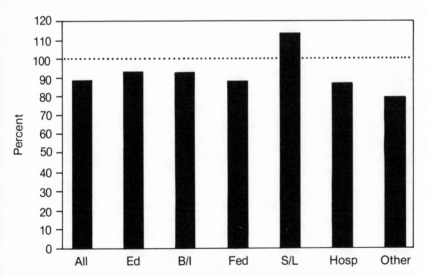

FIGURE 4.6   Salaries of Black Ph.D.s (as a Percentage of Salaries of White Ph.D.s, 1985)

and engineering fields to blacks who were U.S. citizens represented only 2.2 percent of the total.

The data also revealed that the few blacks possessing such degrees are clustered in psychology, the social sciences, and the life sciences. Blacks in 1985 constituted only one-half of one percent of the Ph.D. population in the more quantitative fields—mathematics, computer science, engineering, and the physical sciences (including physics and chemistry).

There are some encouraging findings, however. Black females have been more successful in penetrating science and engineering fields at the Ph.D. level. In 1985 these females constituted almost 3 percent of the female science and engineering doctorate population. The higher penetration rates for black females at the doctorate level are evident in each major field, including the quantitative fields.

The origins of the relatively low rates of participation by blacks lie in a wide variety of experiences and behavior. Among these is their relatively high rate of attrition from the educational pipeline, which in turn has been attributed to the inferior quality of their precollege schooling—reflected in part by the relatively smaller number of black high school students who have been taking advanced courses in science and mathematics.

Another factor that has been suggested as an explanation is blacks' disadvantaged economic status. The average income of black families is significantly lower than the average income of white families. Moreover, the survey data examined in this study revealed that the percentage reporting federal sources of financial support for new Ph.D. awardees has been declining for both blacks and whites, but that the decline has been relatively greater for blacks. These economic forces may also explain why blacks, on average, take longer to complete the requirements for a Ph.D. than do whites.

In addition to economic forces, potential black scientists and engineers may be discouraged by what they perceive to be relatively poor job prospects after receipt of the Ph.D. The data derived from the surveys revealed that the percentage of new black Ph.D. awardees with definite employment plans at the time they receive their degrees has been declining and that the rate of decline was greater for blacks than for comparable whites.

The data also reveal that these blacks are more likely to report that they are being underutilized—that is, that they are either unemployed, employed part time but seeking full-time work, or employed in a nonscience or nonengineering job because science or engineering jobs were not available. This underutilization was heavily concentrated among black males in the fields of psychology and the social sciences. Black females were less likely to report underutilization than either comparable white females or black males.

Once they settle into their science and engineering careers, black Ph.D.s seem to have about the same type of employment profile as comparable whites. Regardless of race, the most important employer of Ph.D.s in our economy is the academic sector. Almost two-thirds of the black Ph.D.s and over one-half of the white Ph.D.s are employed in academia. The other sectors are becoming increasingly more important, however. For blacks the growth in nonacademic employment is occurring in state and local governments and nonprofit organizations; for whites the growth is occurring in the industrial sector.

Given the similarity in their employment distribution by sector of the economy, it is not surprising that, within fields, black and white Ph.D.s engage in similar types of activities. In the quantitative fields (physical sciences, mathematics, engineering, and computer sciences) the most important activity is research and development. In psychology it is consulting and professional services. And in the life and social sciences it is generally teaching. Teaching has been declining in importance over time, while consulting and professional services have been increasing.

Within the academic sector, black Ph.D.s are less likely to be tenured and less likely to hold the rank of full professor. This finding is not significantly altered when the data are separated by field. Regardless of race, the proportion with tenure has been declining over time for females and increasing for males.

Salaries of Ph.D.s have been rising—by about 5.5 percent per year since 1975 for blacks, and by about 6.5 percent per year for whites. As a result, the salary differential between blacks and whites has widened from less than 5 percent in 1975 to about 12 percent in 1985. Much of this black/white difference is explicable by differences in years of experience or sector of employment. When separated by years of experience, for example, the 1985 differentials narrow considerably; there is virtually no differential for Ph.D.s with less than ten years of experience, and the differential for more experienced Ph.D.s is about 5 percent, favoring whites. Similarly, within sector, black/white differences in 1985 salaries range from 2 to 7 percent.

The views expressed in this paper are solely those of the author. They should not be construed as those of the National Research Council.

STRATEGIES FOR INCREASED PARTICIPATION

5

Intervention Programs:
Three Case Studies

Explanations for low black participation in math and science include such factors as lack of career awareness, poor course counseling, expectations of poor performance on the part of teachers and counselors, low levels of persistence, lack of role models, a negative image of science as a career, lack of early exposure to science, and lack of involvement with science-oriented projects (Rowe 1977). In this volume, Davis identifies the key variables affecting the math achievement of black students as course enrollment, academic tracking, and self-concept. Many of these problems are best addressed at the pre–high school and high school level since they result in blacks' failure to choose science or math courses that would help to develop the skills to prepare them for a career in these fields. Research has shown that this is the period of greatest growth in the science talent pool, and that after high school the net movement is out of rather than into the pool (Berryman 1983).

Intervention efforts aimed at pre–high school and high school students address many of these problems by providing career-awareness information, exposure to successful minority role models, instruction in math and science, opportunities for hands-on experiences in science, counseling regarding course requirements, involvement of parents, and activities to increase study and test-taking skills (Clewell, Thorpe, and Anderson 1987; Malcom 1984). Although most intervention efforts have targeted high school and undergraduate students, increasing attention has been focused on addressing the problems earlier in the pipeline—in junior high school, middle school, and even elementary school. A search for currently operating intervention programs targeted at

Support for this research by the Educational Testing Service is gratefully acknowledged. I also wish to thank the directors, staff, and student participants of the three study programs for their time and assistance.

students in grades four through eight, however, revealed that relatively few existed and that these tended to serve junior high school students rather than students in lower grades (Clewell, Thorpe, and Anderson 1987; Lockheed et al. 1985).

At the undergraduate and graduate levels, intervention strategies should focus on decreasing the attrition of blacks from mathematics and science fields, since increasing the pool at this point is unlikely. These strategies—centered around keeping students in school and enrolled in math and science majors—include academic assistance in math and science courses, exposure to role models, academic counseling, assistance with study skills, test preparation and application strategies, activities to increase study skills, opportunities to participate in research projects with peers and professors, and financial assistance.

A recent study of the effectiveness of intervention programs for increasing minority enrollment in medical school (Baratz et al. 1985) found that, holding MCAT scores constant, minority students who participate in these programs have a better chance of acceptance in medical school than those who do not. The study recommended that interventions be made available earlier in the pipeline, particularly at the junior high and high school level, since intervention at the college level exclusively may be "too little too late."

The following case studies describe three programs that serve black students primarily. Project Interface focuses its activities on junior high school students, Project SOAR works with high school students from grades nine to twelve, and the Undergraduate Math/Science Workshops component of the Professional Development Program assists undergraduate math and science majors in their freshman and sophomore years. These programs have been chosen because each targets students at a different point in the pipeline; together they span the pipeline from junior high school through the sophomore year of college. Each program uses intervention approaches appropriate for the population it serves, has pioneered a unique approach to intervention, and has a proven record of success. Because there are so few programs that serve students in the grades before junior high school, a program representing this segment of the educational pipeline was not included. The case studies are based on site visits to programs and interviews with program staff, participants, and participants' parents. All quotes in the case studies are from the interviews; interviewees were assured that they would not be identified by name.

Project Interface

Project Interface is a mathematics and science tutorial program that serves high-potential junior high school students. The project began under the joint leadership and support of the Allen Temple Baptist Church in Oakland, California, and the Northern California Council of Black Professional Engineers (NCCBPE), whose members were concerned about the lack of services available for junior high school students. This target population was chosen because the program's sponsors thought that services offered after the eighth grade often came too late to help many potentially successful students.

The project's initial funding came from a two-year grant (1982–1984) from the Minority Institutions Science Improvement Program (MISIP). It is now supported solely by funds raised from corporations, foundations, and individual contributions. The project's advisory board, which is made up of representatives of the public and private sectors, is responsible for the direction and management of the project. A full-time director oversees the day-to-day operation of the program, which is located at the Allen Temple Baptist Church.

The project serves seventh, eighth, and ninth grade students from East Oakland schools who are not currently enrolled in college preparatory courses, but who demonstrate potential to achieve. Students are recommended by school staff and upon the request of parents. The project goals are 1) to increase the number of minority students in science- and math-related fields; 2) to produce better prepared, more confident minority math and science students; and 3) to expose minority junior high and community college students to mathematics, science, and engineering, to the practicality of these disciplines, and to the many possibilities that the study of these disciplines affords. Students who are admitted to the program participate in rigorous small-group tutorial sessions and field trips, have access to academic and career counseling and to role models and mentors, and become eligible for scholarships and for other programs.

Tutorial sessions form the core of program activities. These are conducted by junior-college-student tutors who are responsible for a group of from four to six junior high school students. The sessions ensure that students first master their current classroom assignments. Tutors assist them in developing basic skills necessary to master the material while reinforcing the students' ability to participate in current classroom work. Once this is accomplished, the tutors' second task is to introduce students to new material necessary for them to learn before they make the transition from general mathematics classes to college preparatory mathematics classes, and to assist them in doing well in science classes. Approximately eighty students attended after-school tutorial sessions held twice a week for two hours. The program plans to increase this to three times a week.

Participants in the program are provided with information on courses needed for college preparatory work as well as with information to increase their awareness of career opportunities in mathematics and science. Students are also exposed to activities designed to help them maintain a positive self-image and to develop attitudes and behaviors conducive to high levels of academic achievement.

As an incentive, awards are presented on a monthly basis for student behavior, attendance, effort, and achievement. These take the form of certificates of merit and are effective as motivators. Absences are reported to parents by way of a "parent hotline": parents are called by an attendance monitor on the day their child is absent from class; on the next absence, the student's tutor calls. The program has compiled a roster of professionals in mathematics, sciences, and engineering fields who share their educational experiences, career paths, and future plans with students. Field trips to relevant sites are conducted by program staff as a means of exposing students to the array of possibilities open to them. The trips are often the result of a cooperative effort with local industries.

A Saturday afternoon computer class was developed by one of Interface's tutors and some parents and was conducted at a local college. The purpose of the class was to introduce participants to computer technology and provide them with hands-on experience in the use of computers. Students were instructed in word processing, and the instructor discussed advances in computing as well as artificial intelligence. This pilot project, which served twenty-seven students, was so successful that there are plans to establish an on-site program that would offer labs four evenings a week and serve all Interface participants as well as community members and organizations.

Located as it is in the community rather than at an educational institution, Project Interface relies on parental and community involvement. For example, parents provided the transportation from East Oakland to a local college for the Saturday computer classes and were responsible for the project newsletter. All parents sign contracts committing themselves to support and assist the students to "put forth maximum effort in school and achieve as much as he/she is able to." The contract requires that the parents perform specific duties, such as "review[ing] my child's homework to see that it is completed."

The program elicits parental input through monthly feedback sheets and holds parent workshops throughout the year. Parents are also asked to attend conferences when disciplinary problems arise. The project director stated that the program "couldn't really function without our parents' involvement. . . . It is more than just helpful. I think it benefits children when they see their parents involved in their education and see them concerned about their education."

Many sectors of the community have given hours of volunteer time and energy to the project. The program has also received assistance from local industry; for example, the Xerox Corporation has placed an employee at full-time salary with Project Interface for nine months to assist its director.

Project Interface has also developed excellent working relationships with the schools that its participants attend. At the junior high level the project staff works with the counseling or the mathematics department to identify potential participants. The project director also works with classroom teachers to move participants from general to college preparatory mathematics courses when the program determines that the student is ready.

Approximately fifteen students were tutors during 1985/1986. They were all mathematics, science, or engineering majors, and all but four were enrolled in local junior colleges. One goal of the project is to assist the tutors in improving their own grades, to encourage them to transfer to four-year institutions, and to assist them in obtaining paid internships during the summer when the program is not in session. To accomplish this, tutors' grades are monitored as are their transfers to four-year institutions. A speakers' series exposes them to professionals in mathematics and science and provides role models and career information.

Tutors receive two kinds of training: professional grooming for the work world and training in pedagogical techniques and approaches. Weekly staff meetings with the tutors assist and reinforce the pedagogical training by allowing tutors to discuss problems that might have arisen in their classes during the week. The speakers' series helps them to understand better what will be required of them in their professions.

Project Interface uses various criteria to evaluate its effectiveness—students' scores on the Comprehensive Test of Basic Skills (CTBS), subjective judgment of participants, data on junior high school participants' attrition, and transfer rate of junior college students.

The CTBS is a series of tests for kindergarten through twelfth grade that measures basic skills and the extent to which the student has developed capabilities and learned skills prerequisite to studying and learning. The test is used to compare a student's current performance against previous performance or against that of another group of students. Students in the Oakland public school system take the CTBS each spring. Project Interface compares its participants' progress and performance on the test to that of other students in the three "home" schools as well as to students in the school district. As assessed by these measures, the project's seventh, eighth, and ninth graders have, in most cases, made gains greater than those made by the home schools or the district for two of the three years the project has been operating.

Responses elicited from students indicate feelings of pride regarding their achievement and satisfaction with their experiences in the project, as reflected in such comments as "I like learning more"; "It makes me smarter"; and "I get a chance to learn more about different mathematics skills."

Overall, the tutors express the feeling that participation in Project Interface has been a constructive learning experience. Not only has the project helped them to hone their skills and enhance their academic performance, but participation has given them a sense of pride in having made a valuable contribution to youth and the community.

The rate of attrition from the program for project participants has gone from about 40 percent in 1984/1985 to 16 percent in 1985/1986. The attrition rates for programs serving high school students already enrolled in college preparatory courses averages about 50 percent. Another measure of the project's success is the number of junior-college-student tutors who transfer to four-year institutions. At the close of the 1982/1983 academic year five of twelve students transferred to four-year colleges, six of twelve did so in 1983/1984, and eight of fifteen in 1984/1985.

Most intervention-program sites are at educational institutions. Project Interface's location at the Allen Temple Baptist Church in the heart of the East Oakland community makes it easily accessible to students and also provides a comfortable setting for their parents, making it easier for them to participate. Church members represent a source of volunteer help, and the program has benefited from this. The program serves students from the community generally, not just members of the church. Only about 20 percent of the students in the program have families that are church members.

A key strategy of the program is the involvement of parents in activities in an attempt to interest them in their children's education and to influence the family's attitude toward education-related behavior in the home. There are monthly meetings that are attended by between 30 and 50 percent of parents. These meetings feature a speaker who addresses an issue in which parents have expressed an interest. Parents also take part in fund raising and planning activities throughout the year.

The parent contract, which was developed by the parents themselves, commits them to supporting their children's education by—among other things—providing certain conditions in the home, such as "a quiet place for [the child] to study," and "no telephone, radio, TV or other interruptions during the home study hours." Parents also promise to take an active part in assisting their children's learning by requiring at least one hour of study time for each "solid course he/she is enrolled in," taking time to meet each of the child's teachers at school, and reviewing homework to ensure that it is completed in a "quality fashion."

The program recognizes that junior college students are a population at risk just as junior high school students are. In addition to utilizing these students' services as tutors, the program strives to encourage them to transfer to four-year institutions, provides them with information relating to careers in mathematics and science, exposes them to role models and mentors in the form of advisory board members, and assists them in locating paid internships in industry during the summer. In return, the junior college students act as role models for the junior high participants.

Project SOAR

Project SOAR is located at Xavier University, a small, predominantly black liberal arts institution in New Orleans. The only predominantly black Catholic institution in the United States, Xavier, founded in 1915, has developed from a college preparatory school to an institution that offers training in thirty academic and professional fields. Of an undergraduate enrollment of about 1,600, half are non-Catholic and 15 percent are nonblack.

Xavier has excelled in the preparation of its students for careers in the sciences. In 1976 the institution's Division of Natural Science enrolled 26 percent of the student body. At that time the decision was made to initiate a cooperative effort to address the problem of underrepresentation of blacks in science-related fields. Approximately 60 percent of Xavier's student body are now mathematical, health, or natural science majors. For several years it has been among the top five institutions in the nation in the placement of blacks into medical school. Although many factors have contributed to the university's success in placing its students into the health professions, Project SOAR is foremost among them.

The program had its beginning as part of the Kenan Science Project, an interdisciplinary mathematics and science effort funded by the Kenan Educational Fund of the Southern Regional Education Board. This project was aimed at reducing the attrition rate and increasing the performance levels of students in introductory courses offered by several participating departments.

In the summer of 1976 a pilot project for entering premedical students was established by a young professor of chemistry to reduce the failure rate of the students in his classes. He had resolved to develop a better method of teaching science, and in the search for effective teaching techniques came upon a few programs based on the theories of Jean Piaget.

Piagetian theory was introduced into the 1976 pilot project, which lasted five weeks and had an enrollment of twenty-six. It was expanded in 1977 to include the departments of biology, chemistry, computer science, mathematics, and physics for prefreshmen in the sciences. The new program's objectives were first, to increase students' levels of cognitive development; second, to review basic reading, note-taking, and visualization skills necessary for success in college; and third, to provide motivation and relief from some of the anxieties associated with majoring in mathematics and science.

Representatives from each of the five participating disciplines developed materials and experiments in their disciplines that would enhance a specific problem-solving skill.

In 1981 the program began working with high school students who would be seniors in the fall. In 1983 the service was expanded to include students between the tenth and eleventh grades (Chemstar), and in 1985 to include those between ninth and tenth grades (Biostar).

SOAR is now a four-week summer program to assist prefreshmen in the health sciences in improving their problem-solving ability. Students are organized into small working groups under a team leader, a former SOAR participant now in medical or dental school. The program has four components: 1) Piagetian-based laboratory exercises to improve general problem-solving ability; 2) specific instruction to improve analytical and critical reasoning skills used in comprehending textbooks, answering exam questions, and scoring well on standardized tests; 3) activities to motivate students for careers in the health professions; and 4) note-taking and study-skills sessions. Pretests and posttests consisting of the Nelson-Denny Reading Exam and the PSAT are administered to participants.

Students apply to the program through Xavier's regular admissions process. Program requirements, however, are somewhat higher than the institution's admissions requirements: ACT scores of 20 or SAT scores of 850 with a high school average of at least a B.

The core of Project SOAR consists of three-hour laboratory experiments—five from three of the participating disciplines (biology, chemistry, and physics)—that stress the five major components of problem solving: 1) identifying and controlling variables; 2) using proportional reasoning; 3) considering exhaustively all combinations of factors; 4) using probabilistic relationships; and 5) recognizing correlations between variables.

These experiments are based on Piaget's theory of intellectual development and follow a learning-cycle format developed by Robert Karplus at the University of California–Berkeley consisting of exploration (allowing the student to interact with physical materials with a minimum of guidance); invention (asking the student to analyze the data gathered during the exploration phase); and application (encouraging the student to experiment further and refine the analysis to reinforce and enlarge the understanding of the concept). Interaction with peers is an important component of the process, which may be seen as a concrete approach to problem solving.

Each experiment has been developed to represent a real problem from one of the disciplines and requires the use of the desired problem-solving ability to obtain a solution. Before they are accepted for use in the laboratories, experiments must meet certain criteria, including suitability of format and the ability to complement entry-level courses, to encourage use of the desired problem-solving component, and to generate student interest. The lab schedule is structured so that each of the five problem-solving components is taught in an experiment involving each of the three disciplines.

Students spend an hour and a half every afternoon, Monday through Thursday, solving verbal and quantitative problems. For the first three days, the classes use a book entitled *Problem Solving and Comprehension* (Whimbey and Lochhead 1982), which takes the approach that problem solving is a skill like any other and can be taught. According to this method, the skill is demonstrated to the student, who is then guided and corrected while practicing it. The key to using this method of teaching analytical skills is to have both the expert problem solver and the student vocalize their thoughts as they solve problems.

Students are introduced to this basic approach the first day of class, following which they are paired as problem solver and listener, taking turns thinking aloud as they solve a series of assigned problems. Listeners are instructed to pay close attention to ensure that the problem solver follows the step-by-step method previously illustrated.

After the first three days, the problem-solving period is divided into two forty-five-minute sections devoted to verbal and quantitative analytical reasoning. The verbal segment continues to use the *Problem Solving and Comprehension* text for the next three weeks, after which reading exercises from sample SATs, GREs and MCATs are used. A vocabulary component is also part of the verbal segment, and vocabulary-building drills are conducted.

The quantitative section of the cognitive training uses the quantitative portions of sample SAT, GRE, and MCAT tests and an algebra workbook. As required in the verbal section, students must work in pairs and solve problems aloud. A few times a week, students must submit detailed written solutions to the problems. This written work is scrutinized by instructors and by the director to assess both the students' progress and the effectiveness of the instructors.

As a motivational tool, a weekly competition is held among the different teams. This consists of an hour-long written test of verbal and quantitative items. The results of the tests, which are taken on Thursday, are returned by Friday morning to group leaders. Then on Friday afternoon all groups gather, and four students from each group represent their team in a quick-answer quiz. The week's winning team is determined from combined scores of written tests and the quick-answer quiz and is awarded a trophy. The team spirit is further heightened by the creation of team banners and other interteam activities.

There are a series of activities designed for students who are interested in entering the health professions. Organized by the medical and dental students (former SOAR participants who serve as instructors in the cognitive workshops), these activities include tours of local health professional schools, presentations by members of the health professions, distribution of materials from the different health professional schools, and small-group presentations on topics relating to health and the minority community.

SOAR has initiated a note-taking and study-skills session five evenings a week from 7:00 to 9:00 P.M. Half an hour is devoted to instruction (based on a textbook) in taking organized notes, while the second part of the period has been described as a "supervised study hall" where the group leaders can assist students in studying more effectively.

Biostar and Chemstar, offshoots of SOAR, are commuter programs that work with entering tenth and eleventh graders from metropolitan New Orleans high schools. The rationale behind these programs is that if minority students are given a head start in these science disciplines before they are introduced to them in regular classes, they will perform better and their interest in pursuing careers in science will be heightened.

During half-day sessions over a four-week period in the summer, high school participants are introduced to the problem-solving approach as it applies to chemistry and biology. Although Chemstar and Biostar are separate from SOAR, the participants share in the SOAR social activities. The programs are run by faculty in Xavier's biology and chemistry departments, and classes are taught by Xavier faculty and upper-level students. The programs have been funded by the Josiah Macy Foundation, and during the summer of 1985 enrolled 115 participants. Area high school instructors have replaced Xavier faculty as laboratory teachers. So far, fifteen area high school teachers have been employed in the program and trained in SOAR methods. Another fifty teachers have attended SOAR workshops in problem-solving techniques.

The program has been extremely successful. Analyses of pretests and post-tests show that participation in SOAR increases students' critical-reading and analytical-thinking abilities. The following are some of the results of these analyses:

■ Nelson-Denny Reading Exam (comprehension): The average increase typically ranges from 1.4 grade levels (for participants who score less than or equal to the twelfth-grade level on the pretest) to 2.3 grade levels (for those who score less than or equal to tenth-grade level on the pretest).

■ Nelson-Denny Reading Exam (vocabulary): The average increase ranges from 1.8 grade levels (for those below the twelfth-grade level) to 2.2 grade levels (for those below the tenth-grade level).

■ PSAT (Preliminary Scholastic Aptitude Test): Students with the lowest combined scores at the beginning of the program (less than 70) typically gain about 12 points (equivalent to a 120-point gain on the SAT).

In addition to increasing test scores, the program has been successful in retaining and graduating students in the sciences as well as placing them in the health professions. And it has attracted more students to Xavier to pursue careers in the health professions. A longitudinal study indicated that SOAR participants were twice as likely to complete degree requirements in biology or chemistry as were freshmen who enter the same department the same year but who do not participate in SOAR. A significantly higher proportion of SOAR participants than non–SOAR participants gain entry to medical or dental school. Also a higher proportion of SOAR students enroll in the nation's most prestigious institutions. There has been a threefold increase in students entering Xavier and indicating an interest in medicine or dentistry since 1977, when SOAR began.

The project has also received national attention. Articles describing SOAR or some of its components have been published in *Change,* the *Journal of Reading, Summer Programs for Underprepared Freshmen* (part of the *New Directions for College Learning Assistance* series), the *American Biology Teacher,* the *Journal of Developmental and Remedial Education,* and the *Journal of Chemical Education.* SOAR's director was awarded one of four National Awards for Excellence in Chemistry Teaching by the Chemical Manufacturers Association in 1981 and was cited by the Association of American Medical Colleges for his contribution to minority medical education that year.

Participation and training of area high school teachers in the Biostar and Chemstar laboratories as well as the attendance of several teachers at SOAR workshops in problem-solving techniques encourage the dissemination and use of SOAR methods in area high schools. The program has also influenced the way faculty in mathematics and sciences at Xavier approach the teaching of their students. SOAR has conducted a coordinated, multidisciplinary effort to introduce Piagetian components into entry-level mathematics and science courses for majors in those disciplines.

SOAR employs a combination of different techniques to create one integrated method of teaching. Although the cornerstone of SOAR's approach is Piaget's theory of intellectual development, it is the incorporation of Robert Karplus's learning cycle and Arthur Whimbey's approach to problem solving that makes it unique. This is enhanced by a motivational approach responsible for creating a desire on the part of the students to achieve and excel.

During the time that they are on the Xavier campus, students lead a very structured life, often working from 9:00 A.M. to 9:30 P.M. with time off in between for relaxation. The program is very strict regarding attendance, and staff have been known to call the parents of those who do not show up for class. In 1985 the director reported perfect attendance on July 4. He told students, "If I see the Olympia Brass Band [the traditional New Orleans band that accompanies funerals] march in front of your casket in front of my office, then you are excused." Yet, in spite of the program's demanding schedule and its insistence on quality work, the students in SOAR seem uninhibited and lively, participating eagerly in both academic and nonacademic activities.

The Professional Development Program

The Professional Development Program (PDP) at the University of California–Berkeley was created by the Special Scholarship Committee of the University of California Academic Senate, Berkeley Division, in 1974. The Academic Senate had established the Special Scholarship Committee in 1964 to increase opportunities for minority students at the university. At that time, the committee sponsored what became the prototype for the Upward Bound Program. In 1974, after an evaluation of the original program, the committee turned the program model over to the federal government and undertook another program to augment the work accomplished by Upward Bound. This program focused on the underrepresentation of minorities and women in mathematics-related professions.

Several of the original members of the Special Scholarship Committee were faculty who had been involved in a professor-exchange program with black colleges before the civil rights movement. They wished to work with the type of talented minority student they had encountered as a result of this experience, and they wished to do so in an institution known for its research excellence. PDP attempted to identify and provide academic services to talented minority and women students from San Francisco Bay Area high schools and in undergraduate and graduate programs at the University of California–Berkeley.

The PDP approach emphasizes excellence and the strengths to be found in its participants and strives to focus on students' real needs. One staff member stated, "Anyone who's coming to Berkeley is going to be a potential leader; and the way to attract them to a program is to push them hard, prepare them for leadership roles." This attitude is in direct contrast to that of many minority-focused programs, which see themselves as being essentially remedial. Participants in the undergraduate mathematics and science workshops, for example, are expected to perform at least one standard deviation better than their white classmates. They are encouraged to enter into the mainstream of institutional life and to participate in departmental activities. Letters of recruitment emphasize the honor inherent in being invited into such a program.

The PDP approach is perhaps best articulated in the reports of the research underlying the Math/Science Workshops design. This research examined the way minority students study and the way they respond to the experience of being at a predominantly white university. As the director explained: "We were interested in finding out not so much how [students] should be taught, but how they could be organized to learn. . . . If you didn't have kids organized, motivated, and prepared to learn, it wouldn't matter what instructional techniques you used; they would all go for naught." This approach forms the basis of the Math/Science Workshops as well as all the other components of PDP.

Research found that many minority students enter Berkeley with less exposure to mathematics than their classmates, and that they are also deficient in study skills. Since many come from high schools with low academic standards, they consistently overestimate their preparation for college-level courses. Unlike their white counterparts, minority students rarely socialize or study with their classmates, thus cutting themselves off from a valuable source of institutional and academic knowledge necessary for success. In addition, many minority students misunderstand the role and purpose of academic- and personal-support services provided by an institution. The various components of the program tailored their approaches to address the problems posed by these findings.

The long-range program goal is to produce minority leaders in a wide variety of technical professions in which minorities are underrepresented. Although the original goal did not specifically refer to "technical" professions, the program founders realized that the underrepresentation was more severe in the science and engineering professions than in others. Thus, the focus is on minority student recruitment, retention, and the creation of minority scholars at policy-making levels.

There are three main components to PDP: the high school program, the undergraduate program, and the graduate program. Each of these has a director who is also an associate director of the overall program. Both the high school program and the graduate program have offshoots—the PDP in the Schools program and the Postbaccalaureate program.

In 1974 the Special Scholarship Committee shifted its focus from the Upward Bound prototype to consider the underrepresentation of women and minorities in mathematics and science. One of its foremost questions at that time was why its summer-program graduates were not excelling in Berkeley's general curriculum and, specifically, why they were not doing well in mathematics. To help answer these two questions, a project was undertaken to do research into the differences between black and Asian-American students and their acculturation into the university community.

PDP staff pinpointed Berkeley's demanding one-year calculus sequence as a major stumbling block for previously successful minority students. The series (Math IA, IB, IC) was the first year of a two-year mathematics sequence that is a prerequisite for all engineering and physical science majors, as well as the preferred calculus sequence for business administration, computer science, and biological science majors. Data established the fact that every year prior to the creation of the PDP Math/Science Workshops, the average grade of black and Chicano students was far below the class average and often even below the university's minimally acceptable scholarship level (a grade of D). More than one-fourth of the minority students who attempted Math 1A during this time dropped the class before completing it, and thus did not receive a grade. Many, after failing the sequence of mathematics classes, left the university altogether.

The Math/Science Workshops project subscribes to the same long-range goal as the other PDP components; however, its short-term goal is to prepare a substantial core of minority students to excel in their course work at Berkeley. The Math/Science Workshops serve four functions: 1) building a community of minority freshmen that is focused on academic excellence and is a source of peer support; 2) providing minority students with an extensive orientation to the university with continued academic counseling; 3) monitoring students' academic progress and their adjustment to the university environment and advocating students' collective and individual interests; and 4) providing minority freshmen with extensive and continual supplementary instruction.

The core activity of the program is the workshop itself. Students attend a mathematics workshop plus either a chemistry or a physics workshop each week. Group instruction is carried on for from five to seven and a half hours per week under the guidance of a trained mathematician or scientist. The students are responsible for guiding another five to seven and a half hours of workshops by themselves. Workshop leaders sit in on the regular mathematics and science courses attended by the participants, and workshop material consists of honors-level work in the topics being covered by the professors in those courses. The students are encouraged to explore these topics in greater depth while also learning to work in individual study groups and build peer support. The workshops provide academic support and enrichment and foster group work in a nonremedial atmosphere. The emphasis is on excellence and high academic achievement. According to one workshop leader, the workshop approach attacks two strong expectations that students bring with them: "One is that students succeed by working alone and the other is that the teacher is the expert. . . . We want them to rely on themselves and others as experts and to work cooperatively with one another."

The program also provides counseling, monitoring of academic progress, and assistance to the student in negotiating the university system. The main focus of the program, however, is strictly academic. According to the director of the workshop program, "All the usual support services are done in the academic setting." Participants remain in the program for their freshman and sophomore years.

The director of the workshops sees one of his roles as "keeping this an exciting enterprise" for both the students and the staff. He was the original researcher on the work that led to the workshop techniques and he continues to think of the project as a research endeavor. He also teaches the mathematics workshops and maintains relationships with the faculty in the mathematics and science departments.

With the exception of a counselor, an evaluator, and the coordinator of the chemistry workshops, all other staff are considered to be temporary, and the director's strategy is to hire graduate students for a two-year period: "The people I get here are not people who would work here as a professional. . . . I am looking for the best [graduate] students and I am looking for two years of their lives." In keeping with the academic image of the program, he does not hire anyone to teach who is not a mathematician or a scientist. Although teaching staff are introduced to the model, they are not trained in teaching techniques. An offshoot of the program has been the Master Teacher Exchange, whereby high school instructors from the Bay Area high schools co-teach the undergraduate workshops as a means of exposing themselves to the pace and content of current university-level mathematics courses while simultaneously surrounding themselves with highly motivated, high-achieving minority students.

The program collects extensive data on students, including their grades, persistence rates, and graduation rates, which together constitute a summative evaluation. The PDP evaluator does much of the formative evaluation of the project. The undergraduate staff meets regularly to talk about its strengths and weaknesses, and the program has been the subject of a number of masters' theses and doctoral dissertations. An unofficial survey of the first PDP class (1978) shows that 28 of 42 (67 percent) have graduated, 60 percent of these in math-based fields.

During the 1983/1984 academic year, the program served 63 workshop participants (56 percent males and 44 percent females; 48 percent black and 52 percent Hispanic). In 1984/1985 PDP offered workshops to 120 students who were enrolled in undergraduate mathematics courses at Berkeley. The courses ranged from precalculus mathematics to multivariable calculus. At least 50 percent of the students enrolled in these workshops earned grades of B− or better (with the exception of discrete mathematics grades). At least 70 percent earned grades of C or better, an important statistic for academic progress of students at Berkeley. Workshop participants consistently out performed their nonworkshop minority counterparts in each of the project's target courses. Furthermore, in many of these courses, the average grade of workshop participants equaled or surpassed that of their nonminority classmates.

The Undergraduate Math/Science Workshops program has helped hundreds of students to graduate from Berkeley who might not otherwise have succeeded. As one staff member said, "It has made a dramatic impact on re-tention as a by-product; it has produced relatively large numbers—compared to past history—of successful math-based graduates." Several students men-tioned how effective the program was in preparing them for the impersonal and demanding atmosphere at Berkeley and how supportive the staff and fellow participants were in helping them to adjust. One student remarked: "When you're competing against people like that [you're] really happy. There are so many bright people in the program who helped me along the way; and at the same time there were some who maybe didn't understand as well as I did, so I got a chance to explain to them, which helped me. . . . I really love it."

PDP's programs are unique in that they span the educational pipeline from high school into graduate and professional school. By preparing talented mi-nority students for Berkeley and familiarizing them with the system, the high school programs create a pool of minority talent to be recruited for the under-graduate program. Participants at the undergraduate level are encouraged and prepared to attend graduate school, although not necessarily at Berkeley. The pipeline approach provides a continuity of support that is an important ele-ment in the preparation of minority professionals and leaders.

PDP is probably the only program of its type that is run and partially funded by the faculty. This has many implications. First, it allows the program tremendous freedom in experimenting with innovative techniques and ap-proaches. One staff member characterized faculty control as the program's main strength: "I think our main strength is that we're not an academic sup-port program—that's not our mission on campus. Our mandate is not the service, so therefore we get out from under what is oftentimes the usual ad-ministrative rut. . . . The faculty are our overall bosses and in the spirit of academic research and freedom . . . the tone is set for us to be able to try different things and be innovative."

PDP philosophy is based on the premise that minority students react differ-ently (from whites) to being in a predominantly white academic setting. This reaction involves their attitudes toward remedial-type programs; their mecha-nism for academic socialization; and their perception of the institution's norms, demands, requirements, and services.

Program staff, aware that most minority-focused programs are automatically considered to be remedial, reasoned that the talented minority students whom they wished to recruit would react negatively to being associated with such programs. Thus, in accordance with its emphasis on academic excellence, the recruitment efforts emphasize the honors aspect of the program, and students are expected to outperform their nonparticipant peers.

The program also attacks the isolation that characterizes the social and aca-demic behavior of many minority students at a predominantly white institu-tion for whom isolation proved an effective survival technique in high school that they bring with them to the university. PDP staff, on the other hand, believe that, "informal study groups common among majority students are vehicles for academic socialization; they enable students both to 'check out' their understanding of university and class requirements and to normalize their attitudes and behavior." The PDP approach encourages students to work together and to form supportive academic peer groups. All students who were interviewed stressed that one of the most satisfying experiences provided by the program was the establishment of lasting relationships with their peers.

Minority students often misunderstand the role and purpose of academic and personal support services provided by the institution. In keeping with its goal of producing independent learners who can operate effectively in the mainstream of institutional life, the program gives its participants an extensive orientation to the university—its norms, demands, and requirements.

The three intervention programs described above serve minority students at different points in the educational pipeline, so their approaches vary accordingly. Project Interface, in working with junior high school students, stresses career awareness and motivation, the enrollment of participants in high school academic courses in mathematics and science, and the involvement of parents in their children's learning process. These areas have directly affected minority students' access to mathematics and science careers. The last of these— involvement of parents—has been shown by several researchers to be crucial to a child's choice of and successful participation in a mathematics or science major (Erlich and LeBold 1977; Fox, Fennema, and Sherman 1971; Rakow and Walker 1985). Project SOAR developed a particularly effective technique for increasing achievement in mathematics and science through the use of a carefully planned series of exercises that emphasizes the problem-solving aspect of mathematics and science rather than the disciplines themselves. The Undergraduate Math/Science Workshops of the Professional Development Program and its focus on high-achieving minority students in a competitive setting represents a different approach, although it contains counseling, motivational, and academic assistance components.

These programs illustrate three important facts regarding intervention strategies. First, they must take into account the place in the educational pipeline of the students whose needs they are addressing. Research has pointed out that different points along the pipeline require different approaches. Second, they must tailor their approach to the type of student they are serving. As the PDP Math/Science Workshops illustrate, not all minority students require the same intervention even if they are at the same place in the pipeline. And third, they must ultimately address a larger problem than that represented by the immediate needs of their participants. This can be done by dissemination of the intervention model as well as by changing the way parents help their children to learn and the way teachers in the school system teach minority students mathematics and science.

The low representation of blacks, women, and other minorities in mathematics and science careers is a problem so severe that intervention is called for at many different levels and on many different fronts. Research on the most effective approaches is needed in order to maximize the return on intervention efforts. Creativity in applying the research findings is also necessary. And an efficient system of dissemination of both research and successful intervention efforts is a third necessary ingredient in the movement to increase the participation of blacks, women, and other minorities in mathematics and science fields.

6

The Benefits of Black

Participation in Science

About thirty-five years ago, the Supreme Court overturned previous court rulings and declared that American blacks should not be forced to attend segregated public schools. Intelligent visitors from another planet could easily conclude that social change on earth, at least in the United States, is a very slow process.

Certainly some forms of social change are slow. The condition of blacks in American society seems to epitomize how long it takes for a system to remove educational barriers so that social mobility is possible for disadvantaged groups. Although this is not the place to compare in detail the historical progress of repressed groups in society, a case could be made that the social change that has begun to produce some semblance of equity for women was not much faster than the increase in opportunities for blacks.

One consequence of being denied access to the full range of opportunities in society is that some categories of people are not represented in occupations and professions in numbers that reflect even remotely their demographic representation. Our society has managed quite successfully to channel people in some directions and to deter them from going in others. The consequences can be illustrated by the answers to these questions: Why are most elementary school teachers women? Why are most university professors men? Why are most nurses women? Why are most physicians men? Why are more women religiously observant than men? Why are most clergy men? Why are most flight attendants women? Why are most airline pilots men? Why are most clerical workers women? Why are most stockbrokers men?

It is not necessary to answer these questions with detailed explanations because it is common knowledge that these are the consequences of social process not the result of any biological or physiological predisposition. Social processes exert their influence in every stage of a person's education and socialization. These questions illustrate the differences in outcome associated with socially approved and directed behavior for members of each sex. A similar list could illustrate the consequence of membership in different racial groups.

While it is known that these processes limit individuals, society has not done much to change the situation. Of course it takes time for change to occur, especially change that requires the individuals who will benefit from the change to complete extensive educational requirements; yet between 1954 and 1988 not much progress has been made.

Scholars know that the scientific community does not represent the various segments in the American population. (What is true for science is also true for engineering, but I shall use the term *science* to refer to both.) Scientists are not different in important ways from the rest of society, although some people may think that they are. The important point is that scientists originate disproportionately from some specific groups in society. Many other groups are hardly represented at all. There is a virtual absence of several minority groups, and women are seriously underrepresented. For the purpose of this chapter, focus will be on the issue of black representation in science.

The thesis is that science would benefit if more blacks could be recruited for careers in science. If there is any possibility that this is true, then the potential benefit is worth the effort to increase representation. Even if there were no direct benefit to science, however, the benefit of having a more equitable society would still make the effort to increase representation worthwhile, because living in such a society would be more satisfactory for the entire population.

The support for this thesis involves evidence suggesting that social processes affect who become scientists, what kind of scientists they become, and what specialties they choose. It will be argued that problem choice is influenced by the same kind of social processes. If that is correct, then it is desirable to recruit scientists from all social categories in order to maximize the probability that particular research problems are not neglected. In addition to the value to science, there are other reasons for recruiting scientists from all social categories. A brief review of these reasons will help to focus on the main issues.

Legal and Intellectual Imperatives

Since the 1960s, when federal civil rights legislation was designed to reduce the level of discrimination in American society, attempts have been made to provide equal opportunity to minorities. Perhaps the best known and most discussed government policy was enunciated through an executive order which came to be known as *affirmative action*. For the last two decades the primary legal basis for attempts to produce equality of opportunity came from civil rights legislation and subsequent efforts to implement programs that would eventually increase the possibility that blacks (and women and other social minorities) could participate in activities that were previously dominated by whites and by males.

In addition to the general legal mandate to improve the conditions of minorities, some Americans believe that there is a moral and ethical responsibility to make our society more democratic through encouraging wider participation in educational, economic, and political institutions. Without the force of law, however, it is not apparent to what extent a purely ethical or moral posture would have produced the changes that have occurred, however small or slowly, since the 1960s.

Aside from the legal, moral, or ethical considerations, though, there is a purely pragmatic reason for society to open opportunities to women and other minorities: the intellectual benefit. Talented individuals are a scarce resource, and any potential that is wasted is a lost opportunity.

Talent is distributed similarly across various population groups. If the most desirable level of talent derives from the top 10 percent of each population group, then it follows that the United States has not taken full advantage of much of that talent because millions of people—except white males—have been excluded. Indeed, if more than the top 10 percent of white males are involved in important work, then it follows that some portion of them are actually inferior compared to the talent available but not used.

That American resources are not used to full advantage can hardly be denied. The critical issue that must be examined is whether the individuals in the various social categories who have been excluded would make any difference at all to the ultimate advancement of science. The main question this essay must answer to support the thesis that more blacks should be in science for the sake of science is, What important differences would more blacks in science produce? To approach this issue, some evidence will be summarized to show that black and white scientists are different in their pursuit of scientific careers.

Choice of Field and Specialty

The focus of this essay is on blacks, but women—as a large social minority—have also been underrepresented. Data pertaining to women as well as to blacks are used to demonstrate this. The argument that a pattern exists that shows that science is not pursued identically by all scientists is simply this:

The participation of minorities in science is different from that of white men. This can lead to different contributions. And it is argued that the more different contributions there are, the greater the benefit to science.

Consider first a difference between men and women. In 1983, according to the National Science Board (1986), women accounted for about one-fourth of all scientists. Although it was a 19 percent increase from 1976, women in 1983 were still significantly underrepresented in science compared to all professional workers; indeed, women comprised 48 percent of all such workers. Not only are women greatly underrepresented in science, they are found disproportionately in several areas (see Table 6.1). For example, almost one-third are social scientists or psychologists; whereas almost one-quarter of scientists are women, only about 10 percent are physical scientists. Note that these data are for all college graduates with science majors; these are not scientists with doctorates. If the data were limited to scientists with Ph.D.s, the representation of women and their distribution among disciplines would show even more inequality.

Consider next the differences between blacks and whites. In 1983, according to the National Science Board (1986), blacks represented only about 3 percent of all scientists. But not only are blacks greatly underrepresented, they are found disproportionately in several areas (see Table 6.1). Although both women and blacks appear to be overrepresented in the NSF category called "mathematical scientists," the interpretation that this field is especially attractive to women and blacks may be unwarranted. This is the area of employment in 1983, and none of these scientists have a doctorate. The same is true for "computer specialists," who may originate from a variety of fields other than the discipline of computer science.

As in the case of women, almost one-third of blacks are concentrated in the social science and psychology categories. The most disproportionate statistic is that less than 10 percent are physical scientists.

Women and blacks who actually become scientists are distributed much differently from the white male majority, but that is only one dimension of social funneling into scientific fields. In addition to sex and race, socioeconomic origins also seem to influence the fields into which scientists go. For example, in a study of university faculty, Lipset and Ladd (1972) obtained information about the occupation and education of faculty members' fathers (see Table 6.2). Although there are no obvious patterns that rank these academic fields precisely according to prestige, there are interesting patterns in the list. For example, medicine recruits come disproportionately from the highest socioeconomic classes. In contrast, agricultural scientists come from the lowest levels. It is reasonable to hypothesize that this pattern is not without consequences in the orientation brought to these fields by individuals from the various social backgrounds. It is also reasonable to expect that these experiences affect subsequent opportunities and perspectives.

TABLE 6.1 Distribution of Scientists Employed in Science

Field	Men	Women	% Women	White	Black	% Black
Physical scientists	20.8	7.2	9.8	17.9	8.5	1.4
Mathematical scientists	5.1	8.8	34.9	5.9	10.5	4.9
Computer specialists	19.9	24.0	28.1	19.9	23.3	3.2
Environmental scientists	8.1	4.7	18.1	7.3	1.1	0.4
Life scientists	27.0	23.4	21.3	26.8	24.1	2.6
Psychologists	7.1	14.2	38.5	9.1	7.1	2.3
Social scientists	12.8	17.7	30.2	13.1	25.3	5.1
Totals	100.0	100.0	23.8	100.0	99.9	2.8
N	948,200	295,800	1,244,000	1,144,500	35,200	1,244,000[a]

SOURCE: National Science Board (1986, 235–36), compiled from appendix tables 3.3 and 3.4.
NOTES: By race, sex, and field, 1983.
[a]This includes white, black, and other scientists.

TABLE 6.2   Social Origins of University Faculty
by Academic Field

Academic field	Percent with fathers who attended college	Percent with fathers having high-status occupations[a]
Agriculture	25	9
Anthropology	53	30
Biological sciences	42	22
Business	32	13
Economics	43	21
Education	30	14
Humanities	43	24
Law	50	32
Medicine	57	39
Physical sciences	41	21
Psychology	41	20
Sociology	34	18
All fields	40	22

SOURCE: Adapted from Lipset and Ladd (1972, 89), table 7.
[a]Based on Duncan occupational prestige scale, divided into high, middle, and low status.

The social conditions that promote differential field selection by individuals can, in the aggregate, mask diversity within a field. To focus on more precise differentiation therefore, it is instructive to examine one field to see if such characteristics of race and sex are influential *within,* in addition to *between,* fields.

Fortunately, some data are available from the field of chemistry. The American Chemical Society publishes the results of an annual survey of its membership. In its 1985 survey, racial identification plus a large sample make it possible to provide some more precise comparisons (American Chemical Society 1985; 1986). Consider first the case of women (see Table 6.3). These results permit a comparison between the specialty at time of Ph.D. and the specialty in which individuals are currently working. Consider the "degree" columns in the table. In several instances, the percentages are close for men and women. Three specialties—chemical engineering, biochemistry, and organic chemistry—are very different between the sexes. The data do not permit a test to explain why some specialties attract men and women differentially during doctoral training. The important point for this essay is the differences that exist between men and women.

Consider now the same issue comparing blacks and whites (see Table 6.3).

TABLE 6.3   Degree and Work Specialties of Chemists

Specialty	Men		Women		White		Black	
	Degree	Work	Degree	Work	Degree	Work	Degree	Work
Engineering	4.7	1.6	1.8	1.0	4.7	5.4	3.3	3.3
Biochemistry	9.8	9.3	18.7	16.0	10.7	10.3	15.2	15.2
General	0.5	3.6	1.4	7.3	0.5	4.1	1.3	4.0
Analytical	8.6	13.4	8.2	14.6	9.0	12.5	11.3	19.9
Inorganic	10.2	6.6	13.5	6.3	11.1	6.3	11.3	7.3
Organic	35.4	17.5	23.3	12.3	34.0	15.8	30.5	14.6
Polymer	2.3	11.8	1.7	7.4	1.7	10.0	2.6	8.6
Pharmaceutical	1.1	3.2	1.2	3.1	1.0	2.7	1.3	2.0
Medical/clinical	1.3	4.6	1.6	4.8	1.2	4.1	1.3	4.6
Theoretical	1.0	0.9	1.5	0.9	1.1	0.9	0.7	—
Environmental	0.7	4.0	1.0	3.9	0.8	4.3	—	3.3
Agricultural/food	1.3	3.5	1.6	3.1	1.2	3.2	—	0.7
Physical	17.8	10.5	17.3	9.2	17.5	10.0	16.6	7.9
Other	1.7	3.1	1.8	3.0	1.5	3.0	1.3	2.0
Nonchemistry	3.8	6.2	5.4	7.0	4.0	7.5	3.3	8.6
Totals	100.2	99.8	100.0	99.9	100.0	100.1	100.0	100.0
N	20,561	17,148	2,245	1,661	17,891	17,891	151	151

SOURCE: Adapted from American Chemical Society (1986, 27–28, 44–45), tables 2 and 13.
NOTE: By sex and race.

Although the differences between blacks and whites in chemistry are not so great as the differences between blacks and whites in the physical sciences compared to other fields of science, some specialties—especially chemical engineering, biochemistry, and analytical chemistry—show differences indicating that social influences are affecting career choice.

The evidence suggests that social influences on the process of becoming a scientist are strong and remain powerful in shaping the selection of a discipline. When a specialty is chosen, however, the social processes have diminished in strength—if chemistry is exemplary—but have not been neutralized. The effect exerted by society on someone's becoming a scientist and selecting a field is reduced at each major decision point. Socialization through similar experiences in graduate training is likely to work to homogenize a cohort of students; yet regardless of similar requirements for graduate students, the initial influence of social processes is only reduced, not eliminated.

Research Selection

How scientists select research problems is an essential element of the thesis that science would be improved by increasing the number of blacks who do research. If it makes no difference who does science—and no doubt some would argue that it does not matter—then the argument is weakened. Recall, however, that even if blacks made no difference as scientists, the benefit of increasing black representation would not be eliminated. To advocate the notion that it does not matter who does science is to assume that sufficient numbers of other talented people will become scientists and therefore ensure its success. If, however, the newly recruited black or female scientist is more talented than the least talented white male scientist (who would no longer be recruited because of finite resources for recruitment into scientific research), then the average level of talent would be increased as a consequence of attracting the best black or female minds into science.

Problem choice in science has both cognitive and social bases. It is necessary to understand how the social bases operate in order to see how opportunities for influences outside of science affect the direction of scientific research. When early problems are chosen, most scientists are assisted in choosing, if not directed to a choice, by their mentors (Berelson 1960). After formal training is completed, the research area is frequently restricted to a narrow range. And even when the time arrives for a person's first position in which independent contributions to knowledge are expected, considerable guidance may be involved, especially when a young scientist joins a functioning research group. This means that for many scientists a real choice in research problem is likely to be based on the type of position and organization. This may sound like there is little flexibility for problem choice until scientists become senior researchers in charge of their own laboratories or teams. The system is not this rigid, of course, but neither is it totally unstructured.

Gieryn (1978, 98) categorizes three types of sociological research that have studied "changes in the focuses of research attention among a population of scientists." One category includes the question of how social and cognitive conditions change the distribution of scientists across disciplines or problem areas over time. The classic work done on that topic was Merton's doctoral dissertation, originally published in 1938 (Merton 1970). According to Gieryn, Merton showed that changing focuses are guided by intrinsic scientific and technological developments and also by extrinsic concerns influenced by military, economic, and technological advances. Gieryn correctly points out that what apparently influenced choice in science in seventeenth-century England is perhaps true for contemporary science. Indeed, to substantiate that to some degree, it is necessary only to acknowledge the current emphasis on economic opportunities in biotechnology, the program of research called the Space Defense Initiative, and the national need for technology devoted to economic development that caused the National Science Foundation to emphasize engineering research now more than ever.

A second category of research on choosing research problems focuses on the emergence and development of specialties. Of special interest is the fact that at first a specialty does not even exist; later it develops to the point of having a name, a scholarly organization, and not infrequently a scientific journal.

Gieryn's third category of sociological research involves industrial scientists' choice of problems and specialties over a career. For example, these studies are concerned with how and why scientists change their focuses or (of equal interest) do not change from one line of inquiry to another. These changes can range from very minor shifts within a problem area to changing specialties within a discipline even to changing disciplines. Gieryn (1978) offers a comprehensive discussion of the various patterns and their characteristics.

The three categories of research on problem choice describe primarily the kind of studies that have involved changing research focuses. At the level of individual motives and constraints on changes, Zuckerman (1978, 81) looks at the substantive and formal aspects of the focus of scientific attention. She writes, "Prior theoretical commitments and technical capabilities direct attention to certain matters as significant and soluble problems; formally, the focusing of scientific attention on certain problems is at the expense of other problems."

From the outset, a scientist has a theoretical limit to the problems that might be selected. This limit is grossly circumscribed by the discipline in which research training was obtained, and even more precisely limited by the different areas in which some expertise exists. Such expertise is likely to have originated either in formal training or in personal development through study. Thus it is unlikely for a physicist to take up a biological problem unless educated in, for example, biophysics, but such comprehensive training would likely preclude work as an elementary particle physicist. Experience, either as a student or young scientist, greatly influences the structure of opportunity in a subsequent role. Even then, degrees of freedom may reduce considerably further opportunities. Thus, discipline, specialty, and actual research experience all influence the range of problems on which scientists can work and the organizational context in which a choice can be made.

Even if these constraints are reasonable and permissible, several questions are faced by scientists, most likely without conscious formal consideration or explicit resolution:

1. Is the problem significant enough to matter to other scientists?
2. Are funds available to pay the expenses?
3. Are funds obtainable if available?
4. Are the necessary equipment and space available?
5. Can the problem be solved? By me?
6. If this problem is worked on, what work must be neglected?
7. What time commitment does this problem require?
8. If the problem is manageable, what could it lead to next?
9. If the problem turns out to be insoluble, what are the consequences?

These kinds of questions involve numerous social considerations, as well as scientific and technical issues. Insofar as scientific research is affected by extrinsic issues, a reasonable hypothesis is that not all scientists will reach the same conclusions about the desirability of proceeding with a specific research problem.

Thus scientists have still another set of opportunities for social influences to affect their choices and the subsequent cognitive development of science. There is yet another consideration about the research process that requires some discussion to advance further the thesis of the desirability of increasing the number of blacks in science. That issue involves personal orientation to research derived from cultural experiences.

Problem Choice and Culture

Scientists go through a process that socializes them to the conventional perspectives of their disciplines and specialties. In that indoctrination they learn the logic of inquiry and how to evaluate evidence. They become scientists during, and as a result of, this experience. But science is an activity far less precise in most of its practice than many people believe. Scientists are not carbon copies of one another.

What makes scientists different from one another? Why do scientists in the same discipline choose different specialties? And why do scientists in the same specialty choose different theories and methods? These are not well-researched questions in the sociology of science. What is involved to some extent is the total experience brought to science by the novice scientist, and some of that does not get neutralized by the process of socialization into the profession.

This cultural residue and its effects across scientific disciplines are not well documented. The argument is not that a specific cultural experience explains the variation in problem choice. Indeed, the many influences on problem choice (such as organization context, seniority, and availability of funds) probably account for most of the variation in choosing research problems. But the idea is advanced here that cultural residue explains some of the variance not already explained by the process of socialization and organizational constraints.

The strength of cultural residue may vary across disciplines and probably has less influence in the physical sciences than in the biological sciences, with the greatest influence in the social sciences. This would conform to the theoretical continuum involving the codification of knowledge. Gaston (1978) reviews the concept and its relevant literature. Speculation is all that is possible, however, because cultural residue is largely an unexplored phenomenon.

If there is no direct evidence for this hypothesis, there are some examples that suggest the plausibility of the notion. Admittedly these come from the field of sociology, but that is a function of availability, not personal bias. Consider first the result found in a review of several studies of black sociologists and their research focuses. Conyers and Epps (1974, 241) write:

> When we look at area of academic specialization, we find that black sociologists are underrepresented in methodology, social organization, and demography and population. They tend to be overrepresented in race relations, theory, and social problems. The pattern suggests that blacks concentrate in problem-oriented specialties rather than in areas that have little direct application to social problems. Blacks at white schools are especially concentrated in race relations and related areas. We believe this concentration reflects an interaction of personal interests and student demands.

A second set of data relating to cultural influences on problem choice involves a study of sociologists who have published research on black Americans. Gaston and Sherohman (1974) examined all published papers in four journals (*American Sociological Review, American Journal of Sociology, Social Forces,* and *Social Problems*), beginning with 1895 for *AJS*, and subsequent beginning dates for the others, extending through 1970. For comparative purposes, 895 articles were selected systematically from 9,119 articles published in those journals. The issue they addressed that is primary to my purpose is the social origins of the authors of research on black Americans.

They concluded that white authors born in the South are overrepresented among those sociologists publishing research on blacks (in those journals). Combining the articles from all journals, any connection with the South—birth, institution of first or highest degree, or institutional affiliation at time of publication—all favored the study of black Americans versus the study of any other topic. Black authors publishing in those journals rarely published on any other topic.

Cultural background of white scholars was one possible explanation for the patterns observed. One of the most interesting findings is that obtaining the highest degree in a Southern state does not produce so much of a tendency to study blacks as does childhood socialization or institutional affiliation in the South (Gaston and Sherohman 1974, 81).

A test of the cultural-residue hypothesis must await the collection of systematic, and preferably historical, data. If evidence did not already exist for social influences on scientific development, the potential role of cultural residue would be small. But at every turn in a scientist's career, opportunities exist for influences external to science to play a part in the choice of research and its conduct. Looking at one problem means not seeing others. Following one lead may result in ignoring another. Deciding to work on one problem, sensing the implication of an observation, or making a commitment to pursue a line of investigation—all these may be socially structured—and so, part of that set of structured conditions may involve the unique experiences of individuals.

Caveat: The Insider Doctrine

Is there a black science? Can only blacks pursue topics relevant to blacks? The casual reader of this essay may conclude erroneously that the intent is to answer those questions in the affirmative. Nothing could be more incorrect.

Merton's (1972) essay on insiders and outsiders, along with Wilson's (1974) reflections on the subject, require a special emphasis at this point. During the 1960s, characterized by increased attention to black pride, some scholars argued that only blacks were competent, by virtue of their social backgrounds and cultural experiences, to study adequately the problems of black America.

Merton (1972, 12–13) explains the social bases of the insider doctrine by showing that it did not originate in the 1960s, although its explicit formulation is of that vintage:

Although insider doctrines have been intermittently set forth by white elitists through the centuries, white male Insiderism in American sociology during the past generations has largely been of the tacit or de facto rather than doctrinal or principled variety. It has simply taken the form of patterned expectations about the appropriate selection of specialties and of problems for investigation.

This kind of patterned expectation leads colleagues to assume that black sociologists would study problems of blacks, and women would concentrate on studies of women, marriage, and the family. Merton (1972) refers to this as a form of de facto Insiderism. But there is a stronger form that has achieved the status of doctrine. In that form, Merton describes the doctrine as a matter of social epistemology that only blacks can understand things related to black culture, the history of blacks, and the social life of blacks.

The doctrine exists in a milder form. It deals with the notion that insiders and outsiders have focuses of interest that differ significantly. Merton (1972) notes that this notion is amenable to empirical investigation: one can compare problem choices investigated by black and by white sociologists. Similarly, the same test could be applied by comparing studies involving the subject of women to see if male and female researchers focus on the same kind of questions.

Merton refers to an early paper by William Fontaine who "found that Negro scholars tended to adopt analytical rather than morphological categories in their study of behavior, that they emphasized environmental rather than biological determinants of that behavior, and tended to make use of strikingly dramatic rather than representative data. All this was ascribed to a caste-induced resentment among Negro scholars" (Merton 1972, 16). Although the study was not especially sophisticated (and it was published in 1944), the questions studied by Fontaine are still the questions to be answered, for Merton believes that there is a theoretical basis to the expectation that Insiders and Outsiders will focus on different problems and will use different categories of analysis.

Taking essentially the same position as Merton, Wilson emphasizes the necessity that truth-claims be submitted to impartial scrutiny, and adds:

To state that the experiences of a black sociologist may be heuristically important in the development of suitable hypotheses is to suggest, of course, that he may bring to his investigation certain values and orientations different from those of the white sociologists and that these may influence his selection of research topics and the manner in which he collects and interprets his data. The values and orientations of scientists are thus important in affecting the advancement of knowledge, but they do not substitute for the process of having their evidence and arguments meet the standards of validity imposed by the scientific community. . . . In short, whereas an individual scientist's unique experiences and orientations cannot be substituted for knowledge in the context of validation, they may play an important role in inventing and postulating hypotheses in the context of discovery. (Wilson 1974, 327–329)

The purpose of this essay is not to promote the idea of a black science (or engineering or medicine). It is not to argue that more blacks should be recruited into science on moral or ethical grounds (although I am certainly in favor of that). Instead, the thesis is that there is a possibility that recruiting more blacks into science would benefit science. I found no evidence to demonstrate a causal connection between scientific advancement and the contributions of blacks that could have been made only by blacks, and I do not know if such data could be found. It could be argued that the possibility should not be dismissed without appropriate inquiry. One suggestion is that as a social process scientific research might benefit from an increase in the range of the cultural repertoire of its practitioners. Some undoubtedly would have the potential for focuses of research and selective attention to problems different from those currently doing scientific research. If black Americans do not have the potential to increase the diversity in science as a consequence of their various experiences in American society, it is not clear where one might find more divergence from the predominately white male, generally middle-class oriented scientists who occupy most positions in the American scientific community.

7

The Future of Blacks in Science:
Summary and Recommendations

This volume grew out of a concern for extending the present knowledge and stimulating additional research on black participation and performance in American science. A group of distinguished and diverse scholars with long-standing involvement and interests on equity issues in science joined to contribute original research. While recognizing that this volume will not address many of the substantive questions that need to be answered, it is an excellent beginning. The results reported herein are certain to influence future research and policy on this topic. The findings point to several critical factors that contribute to the underrepresentation of blacks in American science. Many of these factors are linked directly or indirectly to the generally low socioeconomic status of blacks in this country. Significant findings are highlighted in this chapter and policy strategies are discussed that may intervene to correct the current underrepresentation of blacks in mathematics and science.

In the Introduction, Bechtel reveals that scant historical attention has been given to the role that blacks have played in the development and practice of science. He attributes this to the fact that researchers tend to view black scientists as statistically rare and therefore not worthy of study, while ignoring the obvious question as to why this is the case. Bechtel documents how racism restricted the ability of blacks to make major contributions to scientific knowledge or to have their contributions acknowledged and rewarded by the scientific community. He shows that blacks have made contributions to science despite having to overcome major obstacles in gaining the necessary education, employment, and acceptance of their ideas.

Bechtel's chapter connects the descriptive data of biographical and sociohistorical analyses to the realities of racism in America and the impact that it has had on the development of scientific knowledge by limiting the pool of potential scientists largely to white males. He then links these historical aspects of black involvement with institutional science to the contemporary issues being raised by the other authors in this volume, especially Gaston and Pearson.

In Part I, Davis and Anderson draw on national data sets in order to provide comprehensive depictions of the current rates of participation and levels of performance of black students in high school mathematics and science.

Given that the analyses by Davis and Anderson began at the secondary school juncture in the educational pipeline, it is imperative that some space be allocated to the school experiences of black children prior to high school. Once in primary school, social class exerts a profound influence on the performance level of black children (Berryman 1985). Many low-income black parents do not encourage writing, and some lack the skills to read to their children. There is strong evidence that many lower-income black children experience difficulty in the classroom because their linguistic skills are at variance with those which characterize instruction in the school. This conflict has been attributed to the fact that teachers generally have their origins in a different subculture than that of low-income black students and their parents (Borman and Spring 1984; McDermott 1987).

First-grade teachers typically classify their students into ability groups based largely on communicative skills. Once tracked, it is virtually impossible for a child to move to a higher track level. The lower the track assignment, the more limited the child's instructional time. Further, teacher expectations follow the child from one year to another. Unfortunately, a school biography may be complete by the first week or so of school, based primarily on a teacher's subjective evaluation of a child's mannerisms and communicative skills (McDermott 1987).

When the school and teachers attempt to socialize students to behavioral norms and thoughts at variance with those of the home and community, conflicts often ensue. The challenge to American education is not only to recognize but also to accept differences without creating disadvantages, whether self-imposed or imposed by the dominant group (Spindler 1987). If teachers have adequate information about the children they teach and their families, they will be more effective in teaching literacy skills. If parents understand the school's expectations, parents will be more effective in meeting their own expectations of their children (Borman and Spring 1984). Together, these findings suggest the need for research that examines the role of classroom processes in maintaining or enhancing black students' abilities and skills (Reyes and Stanic 1988). This is extremely important because of the overrepresentation of blacks in poorly staffed and underfinanced public schools.

In a study of the cognitive skills of four- and five-year-old black and white students from middle- and lower-class families, Ginsburg and Russell (1981) concluded that all of the students entered school with prerequisite cognitive skills for adequate performance in mathematics. Similar conclusions were reached by Yando, Seitz, and Zigler (1979), who found that students differing in race and socioeconomic status enter school with the potential to succeed in mathematics. Despite black students' early positive attitudes toward and experiences with mathematics and science introduction, they later turn away or are pushed away from such instruction in disproportionate numbers.

In a book chronicling her mathematics teaching experiences, Eleanor Wilson Orr (1987) contends that the difficulty her black students were having with mathematics was not so much in decimals and denominators as it was in specific language skills. According to Orr, black English lacks the prepositions, conjunctions, and relative pronouns necessary to communicate effectively quantitative mathematics and science concepts. As a result, she views black English as an impediment to black students' success in mathematics and science.

The core of Orr's argument is that the differences between black English and standard English actually lead to the misunderstanding of quantitative ideas. To make quantitative comparisons, she asserts, prepositions are required in mathematics. For example, in subtraction there is *from* and *between*; in distance, *from*, *to*, and *between*; and in division, *by* and *into*.

She believes that it is good that the wide gap between the achievement scores of black and white students is exposed: the more facts are available, the better the chance that effective solutions will be found. She points out that black students' achievement scores rise during elementary school, but decline 9 to 15 percent between the sixth and eleventh grades, while white students' scores remain stable and high across all grades. Orr believes that high school scores will continue to drop for many black students until the implications of language differences are addressed. Until then, many young black students will continue to drop out of high school mathematics and science. She concludes that much of the problem is correctable even as late as high school. Only an image will be altered by adjusting the course work to lessen student failure. Instead, the work must become more challenging so that students will have to puzzle through the possibilities. At that point, right ideas will develop and wrong ideas will become apparent to students.

Orr thus contributes to our understanding of another piece of the puzzle regarding black students' underachievement in mathematics and science. However, before any substantive conclusions can be drawn, considerably more research is needed on the relationship between language and mathematics (and science) achievement. Unfortunately, Orr does not pay adequate attention to the implications of her career experiences for teacher training. Specifically, teachers must become more cognizant of the fact that *different* does not mean *inferior* in regard to linguistic styles. The challenge for teachers of students who speak black English is to devise techniques by which they can more effectively teach mathematical or scientific concepts. The students, however, must become proficient in standard English before they are taught mathematical and scientific concepts. In addition to the increasing use of competency tests for teachers and administrators, schools must also screen personnel for any attitudes that would limit student achievement.

It cannot be emphasized strongly enough that the education of young black children is not the sole responsibility of the schools. Some black leaders, educators, and parents have attributed the disparities in black and white student achievement to the schools, arguing that the schools have failed to challenge and educate black students, while others point to extraschool factors, such as low family income and various social ills. Regardless, the causes and solutions must be shared equally by families, communities, and school officials (*Durham Sun* 1988).

If black participation and performance in science is to improve significantly, black parents (especially those who are economically disadvantaged) will have to play a more active role in any such efforts. These parents must be made more aware of the economic opportunities available in scientific and technical fields. Low-income black parents must demand more not only from their children but also from their children's teachers. All too often these parents stay away from schools because they feel intimidated by them, the net result being low teacher and parental expectations that stifle the academic performance of the children (Pearson 1987b; *Durham Sun* 1988). Teachers can and do make a difference in student achievement. In fact, next to family members, the mathematics and science vocational interests of young black children are most influenced by teachers (Pearson 1985).

Prior to high school, most students in this country have limited opportunity for elective study in mathematics or science. Students' prospects for enrolling in an academic track in high school (where they are likely to take advanced mathematics and science courses) are enhanced by high achievement in junior high school and by taking academically oriented courses when permitted to do so. Thus, academic experiences during the primary grades may have the greatest consequence for subsequent achievement. In short, researchers and policymakers should pay more attention to the relationship between mathematics and science instruction and black student achievement. Grouping practices that begin in the primary grades may prove to be relevant to black students' prospects for later success, especially in mathematics and science (Alexander and Cook 1982). In general, students who do well in mathematics and science early in their educational experience are more likely to take more advanced courses in these subjects. It is even more important to focus research and intervention programs on these early years.

Many black students (especially those from low-income families) who may have an interest in science and technical careers are first-generation college students. Thus, they may seldom have had the opportunity to meet and be exposed to blacks who work in these fields. As a result, their knowledge regarding the steps involved in gaining entrance into these careers is probably limited. Educators can and should be instrumental in filling this knowledge gap by encouraging community leaders to join with them to form information networks and establish a resource speakers' series utilizing role models. It would be reassuring to black students to see blacks who are successful in their careers (White 1984).

In Chapter 1, Davis's analyses reveal a number of striking discoveries. First, increases in black student mathematics achievement have been confined largely to rote memory and quick recall. Second, there was the predicted association between advanced mathematics course taking and mathematics proficiency. Third, black students attending predominantly white schools perform somewhat higher on tests of measured mathematical ability than those at predominantly black schools. And fourth, the black/white mathematics achievement gap has not narrowed measurably.

The second part of Davis's chapter focuses on computer education, and she reports findings similar to those of the black experience in high school mathematics. She found evidence of computer inequities among the nation's high schools: not surprisingly, schools that come up short are those located in low-income neighborhoods where they are likely to have predominantly black student populations. Finally, Davis relates that black students are more likely to use computers for drill and practice rather than for programming.

In Chapter 2, Anderson points out a number of important findings regarding black participation and performance in high school science. While the number of blacks taking science courses is about equal to the national average, they are below the national norm in the proportion taking advanced courses, such as chemistry and physics. College-bound black seniors score about 68 points below the national average on achievement tests in physics, biology, and chemistry. Black students are less likely than their white peers to have visited a planetarium or zoo or witnessed relevant events, such as animal birth. Black students not only indicate less confidence in their ability to do science but they also are less convinced of the benefits of science to society. Black students are less supportive of scientific research and are less aware of the methods and philosophies of science.

Researchers and policymakers must be mindful of the fact that within-group mathematics achievement differences are often more striking than between-group variations. Most gender differences do not emerge until around the seventh grade. After this time, males tend to show a slight mathematics achievement advantage. However, these differences appear to be due more to sociological than biological factors. Many teachers view mathematics and science as primarily white male domains. Unfortunately, such attitudes are likely to be transmitted to students. Further, most advanced mathematics and science courses in high school are taught by males (Basow 1986).

In this volume, we have seen that early patterns of gender differences in mathematics and science achievement persist throughout the educational pipeline. Any intervention strategies to increase black participation and performance in mathematics and science must take note of these differences. Moreover, our understanding of the emergence and persistence of these variations remains incomplete.

Given Davis's and Anderson's findings that taking advanced mathematics and science courses is related to achievement in these fields provides a sound basis for policy. Consequently, strategies must address ways in which both male and female black students can be encouraged to take more courses that are more advanced. If students take more advanced courses, it is likely that the gap between them and their white counterparts will narrow appreciably. Furthermore, black students' current course-taking behavior serves as a barrier to their entry into the mathematics and science pool.

Marrett's (1987) review of mathematics achievement data confirms that black students have made more advances on "lower-order" than "higher-order" skills. She interpreted this as signaling the success of attempts to teach the basics. But this also calls for more knowledge about cognitive styles because too many questions remain unanswered. Why have similar black student gains not been made in the development of analytical skills and the application of mathematical operations to nonroutine problems? What factors underlie the difficulties that many black students have in solving multistep problems? Marrett argues that black students learn what they are taught. Clearly, then, more needs to be known about the effectiveness with which teachers are imparting higher-order mathematical skills in their classrooms.

Perhaps at the root of the barriers that confront many black students is limited access to quality schooling. There is every reason to believe that black students are not now receiving, nor are they likely in the near future to receive, the same quality of education as their white counterparts. It has been demonstrated that black students attending predominantly white high schools tend to have higher achievement scores than their peers in predominantly black high schools, especially in mathematics. This is not surprising considering that black students continue to be overrepresented in racially segregated high schools characterized by inadequate financing, poorly trained and often inexperienced teachers, and a greater number of teachers working outside of their areas of specialty. In most desegregated high schools, mathematics and science classes tend to be racially segregated due to curriculum tracking. For example, one-third of black students attending public schools but two-fifths of their white counterparts are enrolled in the academic track (Nettles 1987).

In a study of the effects of high school tracking on status maintenance, Vanfossen, Jones, and Spade (1987) analyze the first follow-up of the High School and Beyond (HSB) study. Many of their findings are relevant here. These researchers find track level to influence course enrollments significantly more than prior academic performance or interests. Also found is a strong relationship between the academic-track variable and mathematics and science course-taking patterns. Specifically, their analyses lead them to conclude that tracking effectively channels students into different areas of study and specialization. Although acknowledging that students end up in their tracks partly on the basis of their performance, Vanfossen and her associates stress that performance is not the sole determinant of track level. As evidence, they point to the fact that a very good student from a low-income background (where blacks are overrepresented) has only a 52 percent probability of ending up in an academic track. Track levels of students are also affected by the perceptions that teachers, counselors, and school administrators have of students' abilities. Students in academic tracks are more likely than those in either vocational or general tracks to report positive treatment by teachers. Finally, these researchers conclude that tracking maintains and perpetuates class status intergenerationally by sorting children from different backgrounds into different curricular programs. Thus, school structures and processes seem to perpetuate societal inequities (Oakes 1982).

In the second half of Part I, Thomas and Fechter examine the postsecondary technical and science training of black Americans. In Chapter 3, Thomas identifies several factors that limit black participation in undergraduate science. Briefly, these factors are family and school socialization; inadequate precollege preparation; school quality; lack of role models and support of significant others; interests, values, and expectations; standardized test performance; availability of financial aid; and institutional recruitment and discrimination.

Thomas also found that traditionally black institutions (TBIs) consistently produced more than a proportionate share of scientific and technical talent at each degree-granting level. She suggests the need for more individuals to be involved in the process of identifying black talent. Clearly, then, this process must also call for a more effective role on the part of high school counselors. More systematic evidence is needed regarding the reasons that underlie much of the ineffectiveness of counselors in the identification of academically promising black students and the tracking of so many away from academic courses. In short, is the problem one of lack of training in dealing with black students? racially biased attitudes and discriminatory behavior? information regarding opportunities for blacks in science? the inadequacies of many standardized tests in measuring or predicting the achievement potential of black students? or a combination of these and other factors?

All contributors agree that dramatic improvements are required in the general quality of precollege education. Most educational analysts agree that the generally poor quality of training that black students receive—especially those in racially segregated schools—is directly related to their low performance on standardized tests. Despite countless blue-ribbon-commission reports on educational reform, black students continue to be recipients of inferior education.

It is imperative that black parents take a more positive and active role in the education of their children. School officials would do well to provide parents with more information regarding career opportunities for blacks with scientific and technical training and how course-taking behavior influences those opportunities. With such knowledge parents might take a greater role in encouraging their children to take more mathematics and science courses. The late William Turnbull (1983), former president of the Educational Testing Service, believed that the academic success of many Asian-American students in mathematics and science is attainable by other minority groups because it seems to be linked to family structures and values. He reasoned that their success suggests that the organization of the school and the content of the curriculum may have less meaning than how hard students are prepared to work or, at least, required to work. Thus, teachers and parents must demand more of students. Moreover, teaching is an effort that must be supported by black parents if black children are to maximize the benefits of their educational experiences.

The underrepresentation of blacks in undergraduate science training, as Thomas points out, is not merely a black problem. While it probably represents a personal loss to blacks in terms of fulfillment and added income potential, it is a societal problem in the sense of wasted talent—talent that the nation can ill afford to waste in an increasingly competitive world marketplace driven by scientific and technological advances.

Thomas's discussion of TBIs deserves special attention. She cites evidence of the contributions of these institutions to the production of scientific talent. This production is even more impressive considering that TBIs currently enroll less than one-third of all black students attending four-year colleges and universities in the United States. The major field choices of black students do not appear to differ significantly by racial composition of college attended. It is not known what effect (if any) the present rate of attrition for black students at predominantly white institutions (PWIs) will have on the production of black undergraduate science majors, or for that matter, on the quality of training of those completing their degrees at TBIs. Much of what is known about the nature and quality of undergraduate mathematics and science training at TBIs is descriptive or anecdotal. It is clear, however, that the majority of these institutions, whether publicly or privately supported, are underfinanced. Currently, no adequate data exist on the performance of these TBI graduates in comparison to PWI graduates in the scientific work force. Nonetheless, black representation in science would be even more dismal without TBIS. Researchers need a better understanding of the training of black undergraduate science majors at PWIS. Too little is known regarding why some undergraduate departments, irrespective of racial composition of institution, have been more successful than others in the production of black scientific talent.

In Chapter 4, Fechter reveals a number of interesting points: Blacks have made minimal progress in the attainment of Ph.D.s in science in the 1980s. Black females represent a greater proportion of all females in science and engineering than black males do of all male scientists and engineers. Much of the black underrepresentation among doctoral scientists and engineers is attributable to attrition throughout the educational pipeline, declining availability of financial aid, and the perception of poor job prospects. And there are more similarities than dissimilarities in the career profiles of comparable black and white scientists.

Fechter's findings clearly demonstrate how precollege and college experiences influence doctoral outcome. Most obvious, of course, is how course-taking behavior at the precollege level influences subsequent field distributions and therefore employment, salary, and so on. Black students and their parents must become more aware of the role that course selection plays in career outcome. On the economic side, blacks tend to be clustered in those science fields with the lowest salaries and highest underutilization rates. Even so, these fields provide greater employment stability and income than most others where blacks are concentrated. While recognizing that many individuals make field choices based on noneconomic considerations, it is equally true that many individuals—especially blacks—probably do not pursue a doctorate without some economic interest.

Although a number of factors that inhibit black attainment of doctoral degrees in science and engineering have been identified, one that deserves attention is recruitment. During the 1980s, colleges and universities have been left largely on their own with respect to minority student recruitment. For example, in 1984 only four of the eighteen states ordered by the federal government to step up desegregation had managed to increase the proportion of minorities in their public colleges and universities. In fact, several states actually showed declines. Not surprisingly, a number of observers believe that the political climate during the Reagan administration fostered a de-emphasis on minority recruitment (Newsweek 1987).

Additionally, some institutions and departments have reputations for indifference or even racism toward blacks, and therefore fail to attract black students. The absence of a critical mass may explain the lowered percentages of black students in some departments. The recruiting success of many medical schools demonstrates that when well-organized recruitment programs are designed to attract black students, they are usually effective. Generally, graduate schools have not taken the initiative in black student recruitment. This is reflected in the schools' failure to produce an adequate pool of black doctorates in science and engineering (Blackwell 1981). But the problem is much more complex than this. The initial medicine and science pool must be expanded so that more black students graduate from college with records that qualify them for graduate school. The critical issue continues to be expansion of the pool.

One of Fechter's most important discoveries is the nearly equalizing effects of the doctorate. That is, when controlling for the effects of field distribution, differences in career profiles of black and white Ph.D. scientists are minimal. Similar results have been reported by other scholars (Pearson and Gaston 1985; Gaston and Pearson 1986; Tun 1986). From a policy and program perspective, black undergraduate science majors should be provided with these data so that they might be stimulated to continue their training beyond the baccalaureate level. Professors and parents should be provided with this information so that they may encourage black students to pursue the doctorate. Likewise, students and their parents should be informed that student loans are a good investment because of the low unemployment rates among scientifically and technically trained persons.

Fechter's study should be viewed as a beginning because our knowledge of the daily experiences of black doctoral scientists remains limited. Few studies of doctoral scientists include racially comparative samples. In a study of the effects of race on scientific careers, Pearson (1985) surveyed 565 black and 722 white scientists with Ph.D.s earned before 1974. He divided his sample into three cohorts based on Ph.D.s earned: 1) before 1955; 2) between 1955 and 1964; and 3) between 1964 and 1974. Data were derived from questionnaires, interviews, and a subsample of blacks and whites matched on department of Ph.D. origin, year degree awarded, dissertation advisor, and specialty. Regardless of Ph.D. origin, black scientists earning Ph.D.s prior to 1955 found few employment opportunities outside of TBIs. Employment opportunities were only moderately better for members of the second cohort. Unlike previous cohorts, blacks in the last cohort enjoyed first-position opportunities similar to their white classmates. Additionally, the number of blacks beginning their careers outside of TBIs rose moderately. It is significant that black graduates of prestigious Ph.D. departments finally received initial career placements on par with their white classmates. The proportion of black graduates of these prestigious departments declined over the three cohorts. Potentially, this could mean a smaller pool from which prestigious departments recruit candidates. Pearson's study was conducted in 1978, and it cannot be determined whether these trends continued.

With regard to research productivity, Pearson finds that whites publish more articles, present more papers at conferences, and receive more citations to their work. He notes that this differential is linked to place of employment. Much of the low productivity of black scientists is related to their overrepresentation in TBIS, where research is often hampered by heavy teaching loads, lack of funding, and inadequate facilities. However, the results of the matched sample show both a convergence and a reversal. For instance, blacks publish more books and receive higher levels of funding for their grants than whites.

Pearson's black academic respondents indicate that their most pressing concerns center around the fact that they are the tokens on nearly every campus committee and serve as advisors, counselors, or spokespersons for the black students on their campuses. All of this, they argue, limits their scholarly productivity and affects their chances for tenure and promotion. Pearson concludes that race continues to exert some influence on scientific careers.

Pearson and Gaston's more detailed analyses of Pearson's 1985 data reveal: 1) predoctoral publication is an important experience for later career development for both black and white scientists; 2) being black has a negative effect on predoctoral publication, which in turn effects career publications, but these patterns decrease with age; 3) for scientific prizes, awards, and elected positions in scientific societies, black scientists appear to operate in a more universalistic system; 4) being black has a positive effect on receiving honorific awards and positions; 5) blacks receive citations for performance variables to a lesser extent than their white peers; and 6) salary for blacks tends to be influenced by scholarly publications, while for whites it is influenced by connections and age.

In a study of American chemists, Gaston and Pearson (1986) found that white chemists are considerably more likely to be employed in private industry, while blacks are twice as likely to be located in government. This suggests that private industry may provide differential opportunities for black and white chemists. Among academic chemists, blacks are less likely than their white counterparts to be employed in Ph.D.-granting universities. This explains, in part, the fact that black chemists report less time spent engaged in research, thereby making research productivity more difficult. Overall, more black than white chemists are engaged in administrative responsibilities; however in the authority to hire, pay, transfer, or remove personnel, and to purchase major equipment, white chemists held an advantage.

Finally, job satisfaction is related to educational credentials, race, and salary. In general, doctorate holders are more satisfied than those with lesser degrees, and blacks are somewhat less satisfied than their white peers. As expected, those with high salaries are more satisfied than those with lower salaries. Unfortunately, investigations of the career experiences of black scientists employed outside of academe are virtually nonexistent, and many of the national studies continue to exclude performance variables in their surveys (Pearson 1987a).

In Part II, Clewell suggests ways in which black participation and performance in science and mathematics may be enhanced through various intervention programs. Gaston discusses his views regarding the thesis that the scientific community would benefit from increased black participation.

In Chapter 5, Clewell points out that although the science talent pool tends to form around the seventh grade, few intervention programs are targeted toward junior high school students. Clewell concludes that intervention programs are needed on varying levels in the educational pipeline, but she calls for evaluative research of these programs so that the most effective ones may be identified.

Presently, few intervention programs targeted toward blacks are located in the South, where there are large concentrations of black students. Furthermore, only limited research has been conducted on the effectiveness of many of these programs. From a policy standpoint, the identification of the most cost-effective programs is important given the limited availability of foundation and public funding. Therefore, program evaluation is essential if funding agencies are to make intelligent support decisions. It is also important to program directors in assessing the effectiveness of their programs and in making strong cases for funding support.

The primary value of successful intervention programs is that they provide powerful evidence that the barriers inhibiting black participation and performance in mathematics and science are basically social and thus subject to policy action. Because the mathematics and science pool forms around the end of the primary school years, it is critical that researchers, policymakers, and educators understand what is effective at this stage of the educational pipeline. This is especially true for black students with high potential but low scores on standardized tests. Futhermore, it is important to know more regarding whether intervention strategies work differently for males and females.

Despite the number of existing intervention programs, a comprehensive directory has not been available for very long. Clewell and her colleagues at ETS have compiled a directory of mathematics and science intervention programs that includes a description of goals and activities and an evaluation of effectiveness. The benefits of this directory for parents, students, school officials, and other interested parties should be obvious.

In Chapter 6, Gaston's main purpose is to raise substantive questions regarding the role that social processes play in determining who becomes a scientist, and of what type and specialty. He postulates that science and society would benefit from recruiting a more talented black over a less talented white.

Gaston believes that problem choice is socially influenced through the mentor/protégé relationship. Because of the socialization process in graduate school, a student is likely to choose a research problem in the mentor's specialty. Gaston contends that increasing the black presence in science would maximize the probability that potentially significant research problems would not be neglected. Thus he argues that science would benefit from an increase in what he terms the "cultural repertoire" of its practitioners. Another issue raised by Gaston's line of questioning relates to specialty choice, which in turn influences problem choice. Knowledge of specialty choice of black Ph.D. scientists is limited to social scientists; the few existing systematic studies on problem choice among natural scientists appear to be limited to whites. Systematic racially comparative data are required on the extent to which cognitive and social factors influence choice of research problems. Yet to be learned is the role that race plays in the manner in which master scientists select their apprentices.

In a study of American Nobel laureates, Harriet Zuckerman (1977) found that seldom did her respondents do postbaccalaureate study with scientists who were unproductive researchers. Overall, she found that a disproportionate number of American laureates had their academic origins in highly selective undergraduate colleges and prestigious graduate departments, where students are exposed to state-of-the-art research facilities and mentors working on the frontiers of science. These "accumulative advantages" propelled the students further and further ahead of their counterparts in less prestigious programs. Students attending prestigious graduate programs are likely to select research problems very different from those in less prestigious programs. However, besides a few biographical accounts, little is known about the research careers of black graduates of prestigious science doctoral departments.

When blacks enroll in science doctoral programs, many choose programs far removed from the frontiers of scientific discovery. To date, minimal research has been conducted on "accumulative disadvantage" in science, that is, on scientists who have their origins in low prestige undergraduate schools and doctoral programs. These graduates are likely to have their first jobs in non-research-and-development settings or academic departments with high teaching loads and little encouragement or support for research. Such an environment probably limits scholarly productivity, and thus the opportunity to conduct and publish research, or to apply for and be awarded research grants or honorific prizes. Blacks are overrepresented among scientists having their origins in these types of undergraduate and graduate schools. Thus, it is important to know about the role performances and career patterns of these blacks as compared to their counterparts with origins in more prestigious schools.

The cumulative evidence presented by the contributors to this volume points to the critical role that the educational system plays in the development of scientific and technical talent in the United States. The quality of education delivered to students in the early years has much to do with subsequent school achievement. As Reginald Clark (1983) aptly pointed out, early school successes are important factors in sustaining educational achievement. Unfortunately, far too many of our schools select, sort, and control students, thereby producing occupational positions that parallel those of their parents (Bowles and Gintis 1976; Clark 1983). Much of this is achieved by means of course and curriculum tracking, the net result being that a large number of black students do not take advanced (usually elective) courses in mathematics and science. From the overwhelming evidence presented, it is clear that these courses serve as critical filters in blacks' access to careers in science and technical fields.

While much of the emphasis here has been on the need to increase black participation and performance in science and mathematics, it should be stressed that the current filtering process imposes other limitations. For example, many college, graduate, and professional school admissions tests and civil service tests cover math-related skills. Similar sections appear on a variety of job aptitude tests. Today, an increasing number of professions—such as business, law, education, and the military—are requiring greater quantitative and technical skills (Kaminski 1985).

The intent of this volume is not to advocate that all talented black students be channeled exclusively toward careers in science, for it is recognized that blacks continue to be underrepresented in most professional fields (such as medicine, law, higher education, and business). As a result, there is a need to widen the major-field choices of black students in order to broaden their career options. We therefore believe that a strong background in science and mathematics (as well as in reading and writing) will provide black students with greater choices and wider options. There is some evidence that this is already taking place. Grandy's 1987 study of high school seniors scoring above the 90th percentile on SAT-math revealed that increasing percentages of blacks are majoring in business. Losses for the scientific community often mean significant gains for other sectors.

In recent years, however, black undergraduate degree attainment in the natural sciences has steadily risen—from 15.9 percent in 1976 to 23.3 percent in 1984. Most blacks earned bachelor's degrees in computer science and engineering, fields that have high labor-force-participation rates with holders of undergraduate degrees. To a large extent, these findings point to a shift in curriculum emphasis that provides a quicker entry into the labor force. This is not surprising, considering the socioeconomic position of black Americans, yet the net result is the lowering of the proportion of black students pursuing doctoral study (Brown 1987).

Even students deciding not to pursue four-year-college degree programs will benefit from a strong background in mathematics and science. To compete effectively in an increasingly technical labor market, blacks will have little choice but to alter significantly their science and mathematics coursetaking behavior or accept roles as untrained onlookers—bemused, indifferent, and unemployed or underemployed (Morrison, quoted in Gray 1988). Currently, blacks make up a disproportion of these onlookers in the form of displaced workers, victims of the ongoing scientific and technical revolution. Even when they find new jobs, they are likely to earn less than 80 percent of their previous salaries (National Urban League 1988; Pearson 1988).

It must be recognized that the problem of the low representation of blacks in American science begins prior to high school. Hirschorn (1988) argues that the problem begins at birth, with more than one-half of black children born into poverty, usually to unmarried teenage mothers, and it continues throughout the educational pipeline. Because of this impoverishment, even very promising black students face considerable (but not unsurmountable) barriers to participation in science. Hirschorn (1988, 27) asserts that "many inner-city black children need to be divorced early on from the aspirations and attitudes they inherit, and given an education that helps them transcend their environment." Among students scoring in the two highest quartiles on the HSB cognitive test, a larger proportion of blacks than whites dropped out of high school. These black dropouts may be an untapped resource for the mathematics and science talent pool (Fechter 1986).

Within the black community, more can be done to utilize retired persons with training in mathematics and science, especially in areas near TBIS and cities. Retirees could supplement the school system and develop intervention programs based in churches, recreational centers, and housing projects (Pearson 1987b). Additionally, black-owned companies (such as those listed in *Black Enterprise Magazine*) and white-owned companies deriving significant sales from black consumers should be targeted for corporate donations. In fact, more of these companies could adopt inner-city schools.

Entertainers, professional athletes, and other celebrities can play a more significant role in the pursuit of excellence in education for black children, especially in mathematics and science. These individuals should join forces to sponsor an "Educationfest" for black children. Children could even be encouraged to read books about mathematics and science. And magazines, radio, and television programming targeted toward blacks can do more to highlight the mathematics and science achievement of blacks and the role of these fields in the future economic well-being of blacks. Predominantly black fraternities, societies, and professional organizations can contribute substantially to scholarships and to intervention programs as volunteers.

Elsewhere (see Pearson 1985; 1986; 1987b, 1988), I have recommended a variety of strategies to increase the presence of blacks among American scientists. Among these strategies are 1) more government and private-sector program and research grants to specific departments within colleges and universities that have a proven record in producing black scientific and technical talent; 2) partnerships between TBIs and major research universities, private industry, and governmental laboratories or institutes; 3) partnerships between two-year colleges with large black enrollments and four-year colleges; 4) stronger ties between public schools and local colleges; and 5) altering the tenure process at major universities to provide more credit for mentoring.

Because racism continues to be a pervasive element of American society, many of the solutions to inadequate training will have to come from within the black community. It must be recognized that self-help can only occur when societal opportunities are created that allow black people to help themselves (National Urban League 1988).

BIBLIOGRAPHY

Alexander, K. L., and M. A. Cook. 1982. "Curricula and Coursework." *American Sociological Review* 47:626–640.

Allendoerfer, C. 1965. "The Second Revolution in Mathematics." *Mathematics Teacher* 58:690–695.

American Chemical Society. 1985. *Salaries 1985*. Washington: American Chemical Society.

———. 1986. *Women Chemists 1985*. Washington: American Chemical Society.

Anderson, R. E., W. W. Welch, and L. J. Harris. 1984. "Inequities in Opportunities for Computer Literacy." *Computing Teacher* 11:10–12.

Ascher, C. 1983. "Improving the Mathematical Skills of Low Achievers." ERIC/CUE Fact Sheet No. 18. New York: ERIC Clearinghouse on Urban Education.

Astin, A. W. 1982. *Minorities in Higher Education*. San Francisco: Jossey-Bass.

Bachman, J. G., and R. M. O'Malley. 1984. "Yea-Saying, Nay-Saying, and Going to Extremes: Are Black-White Differences in Survey Results Due to Response Styles?" *Public Opinion Quarterly* 48:409–427.

Baker, H. E. 1913. *The Colored Inventor*. Reprint, New York: Arno Press, 1969.

———. 1917. "The Negro in the Field of Invention." *Journal of Negro History* 2:21–36.

Ballard, A. B. 1973. *The Education of Black Folk: The Afro-American Struggle for Knowledge in White America*. New York: Harper and Row.

Baratz, J. C., M. S. Ficklen, B. King, and P. Rosenbaum. 1985. *Who Is Going to Medical School? A Look at the 1984–85 Underrepresented Minority Medical School Application Pool*. Princeton: Educational Testing Service.

Baratz, J. C., M. E. Goertz, and B. Anderson. 1985. *A Profile of America's Students and Schools, 1983–1984*. Princeton: Educational Testing Service.

Bardolph, R. 1955. "Social Origins of Distinguished Negroes, 1770–1865." *Journal of Negro History* 40:211–249.

Basow, S. A. 1986. *Gender Stereotypes*. Pacific Grove, Calif.: Brooks/Cole.

Beale, H. K. 1975. "The Education of Negroes before the Civil War." In *The American Experience in Education*, ed. J. Barnard and D. Bruner, 85–97. New York: Franklin Watts.

Beane, D. B. 1985. *Mathematics and Science: Critical Filters for the Future of Minority Students*. Washington: American University Mid-Atlantic Center for Race Equity.

Bechtel, H. K. 1986. "Edward Alexander Bouchet: America's First Black Doctorate." Paper read at the annual meeting of the Mid-South Sociological Association, Jackson, Mississippi.

Becker, H. J. 1983. *National Survey of School Uses of Microcomputers,* no. 3. Baltimore: Johns Hopkins University.

Berelson, B. 1960. *Graduate Education in the United States.* New York: McGraw-Hill.

Berryman, S. F. 1983. *Who Will Do Science? Trends and Their Causes in Minority and Female Representation among Holders of Advanced Degrees in Science and Mathematics.* New York: Rockefeller Foundation.

———. 1985. "Minorities and Women in Mathematics and Science: Who Chooses These Fields and Why?" Paper read at the meeting of the American Association for the Advancement of Science, Los Angeles, Calif.

Biemiller, L. 1982. "Board Says Minority-Group Scores Helped Push Up Average on SAT." *Chronicle of Higher Education* 25 (10): 10.

Blackwell, J. E. 1981. *Mainstreaming Outsiders: The Production of Black Professionals.* Bayside, N.Y.: General Hall.

Bloom, B. A. 1976. *Human Characteristics and School Learning.* New York: McGraw-Hill.

Blosser, P. E. 1984. "What Research Says: Achievement in Science." *School Science and Mathematics* 84:514–521.

Bond, H. M. 1934. *The Education of the Negro in the American Social Order.* New York: Prentice-Hall.

———. 1969. *Negro Education in Alabama: A Study in Cotton and Steel.* New York: Atheneum.

Borman, K. M., and J. H. Spring. 1984. *Schools in Central Cities: Structure and Process.* New York: Longman.

Bowles, S., and H. Gintis. 1976. *Schooling in Capitalist America.* New York: Basic Books.

Brawley, B. 1970. *A Social History of the American Negro.* New York: Macmillan.

Bromery, R. W. 1981. "An Example of Student Retention for Minority Engineering Programs." In *Black Students in Higher Education: Conditions and Experiences in the 1970s,* ed. G. E. Thomas. 253–260. Westport, Conn.: Greenwood.

Brown, S. V. 1987. *Minorities in the Graduate Education Pipeline.* Princeton: Educational Testing Service.

Carpenter, T. P., M. K. Corbitt, H. S. Kepner, M. M. Linquist and R. E. Reys. 1980. "National Assessment." In *Mathematics Education Research: Implications of the 80s,* ed. E. Fennema, 22–38. Washington: Association of Supervision and Curriculum Development.

Chipman, S. F., and V. G. Thomas. 1984. *The Participation of Women and Minorities in Mathematical, Scientific, and Technical Fields.* Washington: Howard University Institute for Urban Affairs and Research.

Clark, R. 1983. *Family Life and School Achievement.* Chicago: University of Chicago Press.

Clewell, B. C., M. E. Thorpe, and B. T. Anderson. 1987. *Intervention Programs in Math, Science, and Computer Science for Minority and Female Students in Grades Four through Eight.* Princeton: Educational Testing Service.

Cole, J. R. 1981. "Women in Science." *American Scientist* 69:385–391.

College Entrance Examination Board. 1982. *Profiles: College-Bound Seniors, 1981.* New York: College Entrance Examination Board.

———. 1984a. *Profiles: College-Bound Seniors, 1982.* New York: College Entrance Examination Board.

———. 1984b. *Profiles: College-Bound Seniors, 1983.* New York: College Entrance Examination Board.

———. 1985. *Equality and Excellence: The Educational Status of Black Americans.* New York: College Entrance Examination Board.

———. 1985. *Profiles: College-Bound Seniors, 1984.* New York: College Entrance Examination Board.

College Placement Council. 1982. *College Placement Council Salary Survey, 1982–83.* Bethlehem, Pa.: College Placement Council.

Conyers, J. E., and E. G. Epps. 1974. "Profile of Black Sociologists." In *Black Sociologists: Historical and Contemporary Perspectives,* ed. J. E. Blackwell and M. Janowitz. 231–252. Chicago: University of Chicago Press.

Copeland, E. J. 1984. "Trends in Black Participation in Graduate Education: Barriers to Access, Possible Alternatives." Paper read at the second National Conference on Issues Facing Black Administrators at Predominantly White Colleges and Universities, at M.I.T., Cambridge, Mass.

Council of Graduate Schools in the U.S. 1984. *Survey of Minority Graduate Education.* Columbus: Ohio State University.

Crain, R. L., and R. E. Mahard. 1978. *The Influence of High School Racial Composition on Black College Attendance and Test Performance.* Washington: National Center for Education Statistics.

Cross, P. H., and H. S. Astin. 1981. "Factors Affecting Black Students' Persistence in College." In *Black Students in Higher Education: Conditions and Experiences in the 1970s,* ed. G. E. Thomas, 76–90. Westport, Conn.: Greenwood.

Cruden, R. 1969. *The Negro in Reconstruction.* Englewood Cliffs, N.J.: Prentice-Hall.

Davis, J. 1986. *The Effect of Mathematics Course Enrollment on Racial/*

Ethnic Differences in Secondary School Mathematics Achievement. NAEP Research Report. Princeton: Educational Testing Service.

DuBois, W. E. B. 1973. *The Education of Black People: Ten Critiques, 1906–1960.* Amherst: University of Massachusetts Press.

Durham Sun. 1988. "Group Discusses Lag in Achievement of Black Students." 12 March, 8B.

Edwards, G. F. 1959. *The Negro Professional Class.* Glencoe, Ill.: Free Press.

Ekstrom, R. B. 1985. *A Descriptive Study of Public High School Guidance: Final Report to the Commission for the Study of Precollege Guidance and Counseling.* Princeton: Educational Testing Service.

Erlich, A. C., and W. K. LeBold. 1977. *Factors Influencing the Science Career Plans of Women and Minorities.* Supplementary Report of Poll No. 101 of the Purdue Opinion Poll. Lafayette, Ind.: Purdue University Measurement and Research Center.

Fechter, A. 1986. "Leaving the Pipeline: Documenting Losses in the Scientific Talent Pool." Paper presented at the Nurturing Science and Engineering Talent Symposium. Government-University-Industry Research Roundtable. Franklin Institute, Philadelphia. September.

Flamer, H. J., D. H. Horch, and S. Davis. 1982. *Talented and Needy Graduate and Professional Students.* Princeton: Educational Testing Service.

Fleming, M. L., and M. R. Malone. 1982. "A Meta-Analysis of the Relationships between Student Characteristics and Student Outcomes in Science." In *Science Meta-Analysis Project,* volume 2, *Final Report,* ed. R. D. Anderson et al., 211–288. Boulder, Colo.: Laboratory for Research in Science and Mathematics Education (ERIC Document Reproduction Service, ED 223–476).

Fox, L., E. Fennema, and J. Sherman. 1971. *Women and Mathematics: Research Perspectives for Change.* Washington: National Institute of Education.

Franklin, J. H. 1973. *From Slavery to Freedom: A History of Negro Americans.* New York: Knopf.

Frazier, E. F. 1949. *The Negro in the United States.* New York: Macmillan.

Funke, L. 1920. "The Negro in Education." *Journal of Negro History* 5:1–21.

Garibaldi, A. 1984. *Black Colleges and Universities: Challenges for the Future.* New York: Praeger.

Garrison, H. 1985. *NIH Support for Undergraduate Research Participation and Bachelors' Degrees in the Biological Sciences.* Washington: National Academy Press.

Gaston, J. 1978. *The Reward System in British and American Science.* New York: Wiley Interscience.

Gaston, J., and W. Pearson, Jr. 1986. "The Social Status of Contemporary Black Chemists." Paper read at the American Chemical Society's Symposium on the Status of the Chemist in 1985, New York.

Gaston, J., and J. Sherohman. 1974. "Origins of Researchers on Black Americans." *American Sociologist* 9:75–82.

Gieryn, T. F. 1978. "Problem Retention and Problem Change in Science." In *The Sociology of Science,* ed. J. Gaston, 96–115. San Francisco: Jossey-Bass.

Ginsburg, H. P., and R. L. Russell. 1981. "Social Class and Racial Influences on Early Mathematical Thinking." Monographs of the Society for Research in Child Development 46, Serial 193.

Goldman, R. D., and B. N. Hewitt. 1976. "The Scholastic Aptitude Test Explains Why College Men Major in Science More Often than College Women." *Journal of Counseling Psychology* 23:50–54.

Gordon, E. W. 1986. "Facilitating Student Academic Development: Perspectives on Engineering Education for Minority Students." Paper prepared for the National Action Council for Minorities in Engineering.

Grandy, J. 1987. *Trends in the Selection of Science, Mathematics, or Engineering as Major Fields of Study among Top-Scoring SAT Takers.* Princeton: Educational Testing Service.

Gray, P. E. 1988. "America's Ignorance of Science and Technology Poses a Threat to the Democratic Process Itself." *Chronicle of Higher Education.* 18 May, B1–2.

Greer, C. 1973. "Immigrants, Negroes, and the Public Schools." In *Education in American History,* ed. M. B. Katz, 284–290. New York: Praeger.

Haber, L. 1970. *Black Pioneers of Science and Invention.* New York: Harcourt Brace and World.

Hager, P. C., and C. F. Elton. 1971. "The Vocational Interests of Black Males." *Journal of Vocational Behavior* 1:153–158.

Harlan, L. R. 1968. *Separate and Unequal: Public School Campaigns and Racism in the Southern Seaboard States, 1901–1915.* New York: Atheneum.

Hill, S. 1984. *The Traditionally Black Institutions of Higher Education, 1860 to 1982.* Washington: National Center for Education Statistics.

Hirschorn, M. W. 1988. "Many Colleges Expect Their Enrollment of Black Students to Increase in the Fall." *Chronicle of Higher Education.* 18 May, A1, A35–36.

Holmes, B. J. 1982. "Black Students' Performance in the National Assessments of Science and Mathematics." *Journal of Negro Education* 51:392–405.

Hueftle, S. J., S. J. Rakow, and W. W. Welch. 1983. *Images of Science: A Summary of Results from the 1981–1982 National Assessment in Science.* Minneapolis: University of Minnesota Science Assessment and Research Project.

Hurd, P. D. 1982. "State of Precollege Education in Mathematics and Science." Paper prepared for the National Convocation in Precollege Education in Math and Science.

Ignatz, M. G. 1975. "Low Black Enrollment in Chemistry and Physics Courses." *Science Education* 59:571–573.

James, R. K., and S. Smith. 1985. "Alienation of Students from Science in Grades 4–12." *Science Education* 69:39–45.

Jay, J. M. 1971. *Negroes in Science: Natural Science Doctorates, 1876–1969.* Detroit: Balamp.

Johnson, E. G. 1980. *Analysis of NAEP Data: A Technical Report.* Denver, Colo.: Education Commission of the States.

Jones, L. V. 1981. "Achievement Test Scores in Mathematics and Science." *Science* 213:412–416.

Jones, L. V., N. W. Burton, and E. C. Davenport, Jr. 1984. "Monitoring the Mathematics Achievement of Black Students." *Journal for Research in Mathematics Education* 15:154–164.

Julian, P. L. 1969. "On Being Scientist, Humanist, and Negro." In *Many Shades of Black,* ed. S. L. Wormley and L. H. Fenderson, 147–157. New York: Morrow.

Kahle, J. B. 1980. "What National Assessment Says about Science Education for Black Students." *Phi Delta Kappan* 61:565.

———. 1982. "Can Positive Minority Attitudes Lead to Achievement Gains in Science? Analysis of the 1977 National Assessment of Educational Progress, Attitudes toward Science." *Science Education* 66:539–546.

Kaminski, D. 1985. "Where are the Female Einsteins? The Gender Stratification of Math and Science." In *Schools and Society,* ed. J. H. Ballantine, 350–356. Mountain View, Calif.: Mayfield.

Kaplan, S. 1955. "Jan Earnst Matzelinger and the Making of the Shoe." *Journal of Negro History* 40:8–33.

Klein, A. E. 1971. *Hidden Contributions: Black Scientists and Inventors in America.* Garden City, N.Y.: Doubleday.

Klein, A. H., and M. N. Bailey. 1975. "The Socialization of Achievement Orientation in Females." *Psychological Bulletin* 80:345–366.

Kline, M. 1973. *Why Johnny Can't Add.* New York: St. Martin's.

Kulm, G. 1980. "Research on Mathematics Attitude." In *Research in Mathematics Education,* ed. R. J. Shumway, 356–387. Reston, Va.: National Council of Teachers of Mathematics.

Lantz, A., C. Carlberg, and J. Eaton. 1981. *Women's Choice of Science as a Career.* Washington: National Science Foundation.

Lawson, A. E., and J. W. Renner. 1974. "A Quantitative Analysis of Response to Piagetian Tasks and Implications for Curriculum." *Science Education* 58:545–559.

Levine, D., and M. Lin. 1976. "Scientific Reasoning Ability in Adolescents: Theoretical Viewpoints and Educational Implications." *Journal of Research in Science Teaching* 14:371–384.

Lewis, H. 1972. "Changing Aspirations, Images, and Identities." In *The Educationally Deprived: The Potential for Change,* ed. K. B. Clark et al., 30–46. New York: Metropolitan Applied Research Center.

Lipset, S. M., and E. C. Ladd, Jr. 1972. "The Politics of American Sociologists." *American Journal of Sociology* 78:67–104.

Litwack, L. 1961. *North of Slavery: The Negro and the Free States, 1790–1860.* Chicago: University of Chicago Press.

Lockheed, M. 1985. *Determinants of Student Computer Use: An Analysis of Data from the 1984 National Assessment of Educational Progress.* Princeton: Educational Testing Service.

Lockheed, M., M. Thorpe, J. Brooks-Gunn, P. Casserly, and A. McAloon. 1985. *Understanding Sex/Ethnic Related Difference in Mathematics, Science, and Computer Science for Students in Grades Four to Eight.* Princeton: Educational Testing Service.

Logan, R. W., and M. R. Winston. 1982. *Dictionary of American Negro Biography.* New York: Norton.

Low, W. A., and V. A. Clift. 1981. *Encyclopedia of Black America.* New York: McGraw-Hill.

McBay, S. 1984. *Strategies for Increasing Minority Participation in Science.* New York: Rockefeller Foundation.

Maccoby, E. E., and C. N. Jacklin. 1974. *The Psychology of Sex Differences.* Stanford, Calif.: Stanford University Press.

McDermott, R. 1987. "Achieving School Failure: An Anthropological Approach to Illiteracy and Social Stratification." In *Education and Cultural Process: Anthropological Approaches,* 2d ed., ed. G. D. Spindler, 173–209. Prospect Heights, Ill.: Waveland.

Malcom, S. M. 1983. "An Assessment of Programs That Facilitate Increased Access and Achievement of Females and Minorities in K–12 Mathematics and Science Education." Study conducted for the National Science Board Commission on Precollege Education in Mathematics, Science, and Technology. Washington: Office of Opportunities in Science and American Association for the Advancement of Science.

Malcom, S. M., M. Aldridge, P. Boulware, P. Q. Hall, and V. Stern. 1984.

Equity and Excellence: Compatible Goals. Study conducted for the National Science Board Commission on Precollege Education in Mathematics, Science, and Technology. Washington: American Association for the Advancement of Science Publication.

Malcom, S. M., P. Q. Hall, and J. W. Brown. 1976. *The Double Bind: The Price of Being a Minority Women in Science.* Washington: American Association for the Advancement of Science.

Manning, K. R. 1983. *Black Apollo of Science: The Life of Ernest Everett Just.* New York: Oxford University Press.

Marrett, C. B. 1987. "Black and Native American Students in Precollege Mathematics and Science." In *Minorities: Their Underrepresentation and Career Differentials in Science and Engineering,* ed. L. S. Dix, 7–31. Washington: National Academy Press.

Matthews, W. 1983. *Influences on the Learning and Participation of Minorities in Mathematics.* Madison: Wisconsin Center for Education Research.

Matthews, W., T. P. Carpenter, M. M. Lindquist, and E. A. Silver. 1984. "Third National Assessment: Minorities and Mathematics." *Journal of Research in Mathematics Education* 5:165–171.

Melnick, V. J., and F. Hamilton. 1981. "Participation of Blacks in the Basic Sciences: An Assessment." In *Black Students in Higher Education: Conditions and Experiences in the 1970s,* ed. G. E. Thomas, 282–293. Westport, Conn.: Greenwood.

Merton, R. K. 1970. *Science, Technology and Society in Seventeenth-Century England.* New York: Harper and Row.

———. 1972. "Insiders and Outsiders: A Chapter in the Sociology of Knowledge." *American Journal of Sociology* 78:9–47.

Miller, K., and H. Remick. 1978. "Participation Rates in High School Mathematics and Science Courses." *Physics Teacher* 16:280–282.

Mullis, I. V., and L. B. Jenkins. 1988. *The Science Report Card: Elements of Risk and Recovery.* NAEP Report No. 17-S-01. Princeton: Educational Testing Service.

National Advisory Committee on Black Higher Education and Black Colleges and Universities. 1982. *A Losing Battle: The Decline in Black Participation in Graduate and Professional Education.* Washington: U.S. Government Printing Office.

National Assessment of Educational Progress. 1978. *Three National Assessments of Science, 1969–1977.* Report No. 08-S-00. Denver: Educational Commission of the States.

———. 1979a. *Attitudes toward Science.* Report No. 08-S-02. Denver: Educational Commission of the States.

———. 1979b. *Three National Assessments of Science, 1969–1977: Tech-*

nical Summary. Report No. 08-S-21. Denver: Educational Commission of the States.

———. 1983. *The Third National Mathematics Assessment: Results, Trends, and Issues.* Report No. 13-MA-01. Denver: Education Commission of the States.

National Center for Education Statistics. 1985a. *An Analysis of Course-Taking Patterns in Secondary Schools as Related to Student Characteristics.* Washington: National Center for Education Statistics.

———. 1985b. *Psychometric Analysis of the NLS and the High School and Beyond Test Batteries—A Study of Excellence in High School Education: Educational Policies, School Quality, and Student Outcomes.* Washington: National Center for Education Statistics.

National Commission on Excellence in Education. 1983. *A Nation at Risk: The Imperative for Educational Reform.* Washington: U.S. Government Printing Office.

National Consortium for Educational Excellence. 1984. *An Agenda for Educational Renewal: A View From the Firing Line.* Nashville: George Peabody College.

National Council of Teachers of Mathematics. 1980. *An Agenda for Action: Recommendations for School Mathematics of the 1980s.* Reston, Va.: National Council of Teachers of Mathematics.

National Science Board. 1986. *Science Indicators: The 1985 Report.* Washington: U.S. Government Printing Office.

National Science Board Commission on Precollege Education in Mathematics, Science, and Technology. 1982a. *Today's Problems, Tomorrow's Crises.* Washington: National Science Foundation.

———. 1984. *Educating Americans for the Twenty-first Century: A Plan for Improving Mathematics, Science, and Technology Education for All American Elementary and Secondary Students.* Washington: National Science Foundation.

National Science Foundation. 1984. *Women and Minorities in Science and Engineering.* Washington: U.S. Government Printing Office.

———. 1986. *Women and Minorities in Science and Engineering.* Washington: National Science Foundation.

National Urban League. 1988. "The State of Black America." In *Social Problems: Annual Additions,* ed. L. W. Barnes, 37–39. Guilford, Conn.: Dushkin.

Nettles, M. T. 1987. "Precollegiate Development of Minority Scientists and Engineers." In *Minorities: Their Underrepresentation and Career Differentials in Science and Engineering,* ed. L. S. Dix, 33–38. Washington: National Academy Press.

Newsweek. 1987. "Missing Persons." *Newsweek on Campus.* 10–22.

Oakes, J. 1982. "Classroom Social Relationships: Exploring the Bowles and Gintis Hypothesis." *Sociology of Education* 55:197–212.

Office of Technological Assessment. 1985. *Demographic Trends and the Scientific and Engineering Work Force: A Technical Memorandum.* Washington: U.S. Government Printing Office.

Olstad, Roger G., J. R. Juarez, L. J. Davenport, and D. L. Haury. 1981. *Inhibitors to Achievement in Science and Mathematics by Ethnic Minorities.* Pullman: University of Washington, College of Education (ERIC Document Reproduction Service, ED 223–404).

Orr, E. W. 1987. *Twice as Less.* New York: Norton.

Parsons, T. 1959. "The School Class as a Social System: Some of Its Functions in American Society." *Harvard Education Review* 29:297–318.

Pearson, W., Jr. 1985. *Black Scientists, White Society, and Colorless Science: A Study of Universalism in American Science.* Millwood, N.Y.: Associated Faculty Press.

———. 1987a. "The Graduate Education and Careers of Underrepresented Minorities in Science and Engineering." In *Minorities: Their Underrepresentation and Career Differentials in Science and Engineering,* ed. L. S. Dix, 133–149. Washington: National Academy Press.

———. 1987b. "The Flow of Black Scientific Talent: Leaks in the Pipeline." *Humbolt Journal of Social Relations* 14:44–61.

———. 1988. "The Effects of New Technologies on Black Americans." Paper read at the Association of Social and Behavioral Scientists meeting. Greensboro, N.C.

Pearson, W., Jr., and J. R. Earle. 1984. "Race-Gender Variations in the Demographic Characteristics of Doctoral Scientists." *Sociological Spectrum* 4:229–248.

Pearson, W., Jr., and J. Gaston. 1985. "Race and Universalism in American Science." Paper read at the American Association for the Advancement of Science meeting. Los Angeles, Calif.

Pearson, W., Jr., and L. C. Pearson. 1985. "Baccalaureate Origins of Black American Scientists: A Cohort Analysis." *Journal of Negro Education* 54:24–34.

Peng, S. 1982. *Science and Mathematics Education in American High Schools: Results from the High School and Beyond Study.* Washington: National Center for Education Statistics (ERIC Document Reproduction Service, ED 249–259).

Perkins, L. M. 1978. "Fanny Jackson Coppin and the Institute for Colored Youth." Ph.D. dissertation, University of Illinois at Urbana-Champaign.

Pifer, A. 1973. *The Higher Education of Blacks in the United States.* New York: Carnegie Corporation.

Ploski, H. A., and J. Williams. 1983. *The Afro-American,* 4th ed. New York: Wiley.

Quarles, B. 1969. *The Negro in the Making of America.* New York: Macmillan.

Rakow, S. J., and C. L. Walker. 1985. "The Status of Hispanic American Students in Science: Achievement and Exposure." *Science Education* 69:557–565.

Rakow, S. J., W. W. Welch, and S. J. Hueftle. 1984. "Student Achievement in Science: A Comparison of National Assessment Results." *Science Education* 68:571–578.

Reyes, L. H. and G. M. A. Stanic. 1988. "Race, Sex, Socioeconomic Status, and Mathematics." *Journal for Research in Mathematics Education* 19:26–43.

Rice, L. D. 1971. *The Negro in Texas, 1874–1900.* Baton Rouge: Louisiana State University Press.

Richards, J. M., G. D. Williams, and J. L. Holland. 1981. "An Evaluation of the 1977 Minority Introduction to Engineering Summer Program." In *Black Students in Higher Education: Conditions and Experiences in the 1970s,* ed. G. E. Thomas, 235–252. Westport, Conn.: Greenwood.

Rock, D., R. Ekstrom, M. Goertz, T. Hilton, and J. Pollack. 1984. *Excellence in High School Education: Cross-Sectional Study, 1972–1980 Final Report.* Contract No. 300-83-0247. Princeton: Educational Testing Service.

Rossiter, M. W. 1974. "Women Scientists in America before 1920." *American Scientist* 62:312–323.

Rowe, M. B. 1977. "Why Don't Blacks Pick Science? *Science Teacher* 44:34–35.

Scott, W. B. 1981. "Critical Factors for the Survival of First Generation College Blacks." In *Black Students in Higher Education: Conditions and Experiences in the 1970s,* ed. G. E. Thomas, 226–231. Westport, Conn.: Greenwood.

Sells, L. W. 1976. "The Mathematics Filter and the Education of Women and Minorities." Paper read at the annual meeting of the American Association for the Advancement of Science, Boston, Mass.

Simpson, R. D. 1978. "Relating Student Feelings to Achievement in Science." In *What Research Says to the Science Teacher,* vol. 1. Washington: National Science Teachers Association.

———. 1979. "Breeding Success in Science." *Science Teacher* 46:24–26.

Spindler, G. D. 1987. "Why Have Minority Groups in North America Been Disadvantaged by Their Schools?" In *Education and Cultural Process: Anthropological Approaches,* 2d ed., ed. G. D. Spindler, 160–172. Prospect Heights, Ill.: Waveland.

Spivey, D. 1978. *Schooling for the New Slavery: Black Industrial Education, 1868–1915*. Westport, Conn.: Greenwood.

Staples, B. 1986. "The Dwindling Black Presence on Campus." *New York Times Magazine*, 27 April.

Thomas, G. E. 1980. "Race and Sex Group Equity in Higher Education: Institutional and Major Field Enrollment Statuses." *American Educational Research Journal* 17:171–181.

———. 1981. "The Effects of Standardized Achievement Test Performance and Family Status on Black-White College Access." In *Black Students in Higher Education: Conditions and Experiences in the 1970s*, ed. G. E. Thomas, 49–63. Westport, Conn.: Greenwood.

———. 1984. *Black College Students and Factors Influencing Their Major Field Choice*. Atlanta: Southern Education Foundation.

———. 1986a. "Cultivating the Interest of Women and Minorities in High School Mathematics and Science." *Science Education* 70:31–43.

———. 1986b. *The Access and Success of Blacks and Hispanics in U.S. Graduate and Professional Education*. Washington: National Academy of Science.

Toppin, E. A. 1971. *A Biographical History of Blacks in America since 1528*. New York: David McKay.

Trent, W. T. 1984. "Equity Considerations in Higher Education: Race and Sex Differences in Degree Attainment and Major Field from 1976 through 1981." *American Journal of Education* 41:280–305.

Tun, S. 1986. *Chinese in the U.S. Chemical Profession: 1985 Statistical Profile*. Washington: American Chemical Society.

Turnbull, W. W. 1983. "Schooling for the Age of Technology: Where Does America Stand?" Statement before the Joint Economic Committee, Congress of the United States, Washington.

U.S. Bureau of the Census. 1985. *Statistical Abstract of the United States, 106th Edition*. Washington: U.S. Government Printing Office.

U.S. Office of Civil Rights. 1981. Unpublished data from the Higher Education General Information Survey. Washington: U.S. Office of Civil Rights.

Useem, M. 1976. "Government Influence on the Social Science Paradigm." *Sociological Quarterly* 17:146–161.

Usiskin, Z. 1985. "We Need Another Revolution in School Mathematics." In *The Secondary School Curriculum 1985 Yearbook*, ed. C. R. Hirsch and M. J. Zweng, 1–21. Reston, Va.: National Council of Teachers of Mathematics.

Vanfossen, B., J. Jones, and J. Spade. 1987. "Curriculum Tracking and Status Maintenance." *Sociology of Education* 60:104–122.

Vetter, B. M., and E. L. Babco. 1986. *Professional Women and Minorities*. Washington: Commission on Professionals in Science and Technology.

Whimbey, A., and J. Lochhead. 1982. *Problem Solving and Comprehension*, 3d ed. Philadelphia: Franklin Institute Press.

White, J. L. 1984. *The Psychology of Blacks*. Englewood Cliffs, N.J.: Prentice-Hall.

Wilson, W. J. 1974. "The New Black Sociology: Reflections on the 'Insiders and Outsiders' Controversy." In *Black Sociologists: Historical and Contemporary Perspectives*, ed. J. E. Blackwell and M. Janowitz, 322–338. Chicago: University of Chicago Press.

Winston, M. R. 1971. "Through the Back Door: Academic Racism and the Negro Scholar in Historical Perspective." *Daedalus* 100:678–719.

Wirszup, I. 1983. "Educational and National Survival: Confronting the Mathematics and Science Crises in American Schools." *Educational Leadership* 41:5–11.

Woodson, C. G. 1915. *The Education of the Negro prior to 1861*. New York: Putnam.

———. 1969. *The Negro Professional Man and the Community*. New York: Negro University Press.

Work, M. N. 1931. *Negro Year Book: An Annual Encyclopedia of the Negro, 1931–1932*. Tuskegee, Ala.: Negro Year Book Publishing Company.

Yando, R., V. Seitz, and E. Zigler. 1979. *Intellectual and Personality Characteristics of Children: Social-Class and Ethnic-Group Differences*. Hillsdale, N.J.: Erlbaum.

Young, H. A. 1981. "Retaining Blacks in Science: An Affective Model." In *Black Students in Higher Education: Conditions and Experiences in the 1970s*, ed. G. E. Thomas, 261–271. Westport, Conn.: Greenwood.

Zuckerman, H. 1977. *Scientific Elite: Nobel Laureates in the United States*. New York: Free Press.

———. 1978. "Theory Choice and Problem Choice in Science." In *The Sociology of Science*, ed. J. Gaston, 65–95. San Francisco: Jossey-Bass.

INDEX

(Page numbers in italic indicate material in tables or figures.)

academic ability and potential, evaluating, 77
academic assistance, in graduate and professional schools, 63. *See also* educational intervention
academic employment: fields of Ph.D.s in, *95;* of Ph.D.s, 90, 92, 93, 95, *96,* 97; rank and, 93, 95, *96,* 97; of tenured Ph.D.s, *94*
academic success, families and, 144
acculturation, differences between black and Asian-American students in, 117
achievement: influence of primary grades on subsequent, 139. *See also* science achievement tests
Adams decision, 69
Admissions Testing Program (ATP), 44, 45
advanced degrees, sponsorship to pursue, 61, 76. *See also* Ph.D. degrees
affirmative action, 125
Allen Temple Baptist Church (Oakland, CA), 107, 110
American Board of Surgery, 16
American College of Surgeons, 16
American Missionary Association, 3
Amherst College, 16
analytical thinking, Project SOAR and, 113, 114. *See also* problem-solving methods
Armstrong, General Samuel, 8–9
aspirations: of black pupils, 51; early formation of, 77. *See also* career plans and expectations
Atlanta University, *73, 74,* 75
ATP, *see* Admissions Testing Program (ATP)
attitudes: divergence between achievement scores and, 55; feelings of pride and, 109; toward conservation, 47; toward science, 43, 45, *46,* 47–48, 54;

toward societal problems, 47; toward socioscientific responsibility, 48

Ballard, Allen, 4
Bannecker, Benjamin, 11
barriers to black students in higher education, 62
behavioral norms and thoughts, 138
Bell, Alexander Graham, 13
biological sciences, bachelors', masters', and doctoral degrees from TBIS in, 69, *70*
biology courses, *50;* enrollment in college and graduate, *66, 67, 72, 73, 74;* to fulfill science requirement, 49. *See also* science and engineering
Biostar program, 112, 114, 115
black academics as tokens, 147. *See also* faculty
black children, school experiences of, 138
black colleges and universities, prime problems of, 77. *See also* traditionally black institutions (TBIS); *names of specific institutions*
black dropouts, 23; as untapped resource, 151
black English, 139
black females, 80–81. *See also* sex differences; women
black graduate students, mentors for, 61, 76
black high school students, mathematics course enrollments and, 23, 24, 25, 26, 30–32. *See also* science attitudes
black inventors, 10–13
black-owned companies as source for donations, 151
blacks: attrition from educational pipeline by, 67; belief in inferiority of, 7; danger of disenfranchisement in increasingly technical society, 41; as focus of research, 133, 134; as percent of people employed in

blacks (*continued*)
  professional specialties, 80; as percent
    of scientists and engineers, 80; in the
    Ph.D. population, 79–82; place in so-
    ciety in post–Civil War South, 4;
    underrepresentation in science, engi-
    neering, and mathematics, 67–68,
    75–76; in white schools (in 1800s), 7
black scientists, 10–16; academic ori-
    gins of, 149; baccalaureate origins of,
    68, 71, 74–78; contributions by,
    10–17, 136; lack of recognition of,
    16–17; as percent of scientists, 19;
    strategies to increase proportion of,
    151–152. *See also* black inventors;
    names of individual scientists
black sociologists: heuristic implications
    of experiences of, 135–136; research
    focuses of, 133
black students: identification of promis-
    ing, 143; interaction between black
    teachers and, 61
black/white salary differentials of
    Ph.D.s, 97–99
borrowing and loans, 63, 146. *See also*
    financial aid
Bouchet, Edward Alexander, 13, 17, 18
business majors, 15
busing, 5, 20

career information and awareness: for
    parents of students, 144; program for,
    40–41, 107, 113–114, 121
career plans and expectations, 61; early
    formulation of, 77; lack of encourage-
    ment to pursue nontraditional, 62; of
    new Ph.D.s, 84, 85; of poor and mi-
    nority students, 44; Project Interface
    and, 107, 108. *See also* aspirations;
    scientific careers
careers: blacks', 145; effects of race on
    scientific, 146, 147; filters in blacks'
    access to scientific, 150; low minority
    representation in mathematics and sci-
    ence, 122; profiles of Ph.D., 146;
    race and sex disparities in occupa-
    tional attainment in, 76

celebrities' role in pursuit of educational
    excellence for blacks, 151
Chemistar program, 112, 114, 115
chemistry: courses in, 49; race and sex
    and, 128, *129,* 130. *See also* physical
    science courses
chemists, race and careers of, 147
City University of New York (CUNY),
    71, 72, 73, 75
classroom processes, role of, 138. *See
    also* schools
cognitive skills, mathematics and,
    138–139
college graduates: employment for, 60.
    See also careers
college-level courses, overestimation of
    preparation for, 117
college preparatory work, information
    on courses needed, 107
college students, first generation,
    140–141
Columbia University, 16
communication skills, 138, 139
Comprehensive Test of Basic Skills
    (CTBS), 109
computers, 20; hands-on experience
    with, 108; racial inequities and train-
    ing in, 39; students' use of, 141;
    training in use of, 39–40, 141
computer science, bachelors' degrees in,
    150
conservation, attitudes toward, 47
consulting as primary work of Ph.D.s in
    psychology, 90, 92
Cope, Alfred, 14
Cornell University, *73, 74,* 75
corporate donations, 151
curriculum(a): course-taking behavior by
    pupils in different, 49, 51; enrollment
    patterns in academic, 30–31; race and
    enrollment in type of, 29–32;
    watered-down, 20. *See also* educa-
    tion; industrial education; tracking;
    vocational education

Dartmouth [College], 15
DePauw University, 15, 17

desegregation of state colleges and universities, 69
discrimination: as influence on minority enrollment in mathematics and science, 63; institutional, 17
doctoral-level studies, blacks' pursuit of, 19. *See also* advanced degrees
Drew, Charles, 16
dropouts, 23, 151
DuBois, W. E. B., 15

education: advanced, 19, 61, 62–63, 76, 83; of blacks, 2–10, 140; funding for black, 5; industrial, 4; influence of early, 150; in North after Civil War, 8; persistence of separate and unequal, 28; of slaves and free blacks, 2, 3; in South after Civil War, 2–5, 7, 8, 9; vocational, 9, 14. *See also* curriculum; schools; tracking
educational intervention, *see* academic assistance; intervention; tutorial programs for minorities
educational philosophy, black post-Reconstructionist, 4
educational policies and practices, blacks and, 19, 56–57
Effect of Mathematics Course Enrollment on Racial/Ethnic Differences in Secondary School Mathematics, 25
electrical engineering, 12–13
Embry-Riddle University, 72, 74
employment: of black Ph.D.s, 84–85; of college graduates, 60; of scientists, engineers, and mathematicians, 60. *See also* career information and awareness; career plans and expectations; careers; unemployment
engineering: bachelors' degrees in, 150; bachelors' degrees from TBIS in, 69, 70, 72; black females in, 80; doctors' degrees from TBIS in, 70, 71, 75; masters' degrees from TBIS in, 69, 73
engineers, *see* scientists and engineers

faculty: control of PDP by, 120; influence of black, 61, 76

families, academic success and, 144. *See also* parents
family-support networks, frequent absence of black, 61
federal initiatives, mathematics experiences for minorities and, 40, 41
field selection, 126
field trips, 108. *See also* science activities
financial aid: academic loans as investments, 146; for higher education, 62–63, 76, 83–84; scholarships as, 107
Fisk University, 68, 72
Fontaine, William, 135
Forten, James, 10–11
Freedman's Bureau, 3

gender differences, *see* sex differences
Glidden Company, 15
graduate education, 19, 61; cost of, 62; financing, 62–63, 76, 83
Graduate Record Examination (GRE), black performance on, 62
Griffith Laboratories (Chicago), 16
grouping practices, relevance of, 139. *See also* curriculum; tracking

Hall, Lloyd A., 16
Hampton Institute, 8, 14
Harvard University, 15; first black professor of medicine at, 16; medical school, 16
health professions, 106; Project SOAR and, 111, 113–115
higher education: access to, 19, 61, 62; financial aid for, 62–63; survey of black students in, 60
High School and Beyond (HSB) study, 44, 45
high school science courses: achievement scores and enrollment in, 43; avoidance of advanced and quantitative, 51, 54, 56, 57; blacks in, 141; choice of appropriate (for enrolling as college science major), 49; diluted, 57; ethnic gap in enrollment in, 51, 56; participation and perfor-

high school science courses (*continued*)
mance in (by blacks), 54–58; pupils'
selection of, 43, 49
Hinton, William A., 16
Hinton test for syphillis, 16
homework, time spent on, 62
Hopkins Grammar School, 13
Howard University, 15, 16, 68, 71, 72,
73, 75
HSB, *see* High School and Beyond (HSB)
study

illiteracy of blacks following Civil War, 3
income, race and sex disparities in, 76
industrial education, 8–10, 14; movement against, 15
inferiority, white belief in black, 17, 19
insider doctrine, 135–136
Institute for Colored Youth (ICY), 14
intellectual development, instruction and
learning and, 57
interests and abilities, relationships between, 56. *See also* aspirations;
attitudes, career plans and expectations; test scores
intervention: director of programs for,
148; effectiveness for increasing minority medical school enrollment,
106; evaluation of programs for, 148;
importance of early, 77; low minority
representation in mathematics and science and, 122; strategies for, 106,
121; volunteers in, 151, *See also* academic assistance; Professional
Development Program; Project Interface; Project SOAR; tutorial programs
for minorities

Jim Crow laws, 18
job satisfaction, 147
Julian, Percy, 15–16, 17
junior high students, Project Interface
and, 106–107
Just, Ernest, 15, 17, 18

Karpus, Robert, 112
Kenan Science Project, 111

laboratories: blacks barred from university, 18; poor, 58
labor market, importance of mathematics and science for entering, 151
language difficulties, 138, 139
Latimer, Lewis, 11, 12–13
liberal education, 14
linguistic skills, 138, 139
loans and financial aid, 62–63, 76,
83–84; as investment, 146
lynchings, 18

McCoy, Elijah, 11, 12
McGill University, 16
management/administration as primary
work of Ph.D.s, 90, *91*, 92
Marine Biological Laboratories, 15
mathematicians, employment among, 60
mathematics: academic high school curriculum and, 28; achievement of black
students in, 141–142; agenda for
teaching, 25–26; attitudes toward, 24,
37–38, 139; avoidance of, 34; bachelors' degrees from TBIS in, *72;* black
doctorates in, *74,* 75; black underrepresentation in, 60–63; cognitive
skills and, 138–139; critical barrier
to proficiency in, 38–39; decline in
training in, 26; enrollment and degree
attainment in, 64, *65,* 67–69, *70,* 71,
72–73, 74–75; factors that discourage black participation in, 63; gaps in
training in, 31; gender differences in,
141–142; GRE and, 62; lack of challenging experiences in, 32; lack of opportunity to learn, 24; language skills
and, 139; low black scores on tests in,
23; low exposure to, 117; masters' degrees from TBIS in, 69, *70, 73, 74*; parents' expectations and, 38; priorities
for education in, 42; problem solving
and, 121; in Professional Development
Program, 117–118; results of inadequate preparation in, 58; SAT scores in,
25, *26,* 62; students' feelings about,
37–38; *Third National Mathematics
Assessment* (1983) and, 29–38

mathematics achievement, 32–34, *35;*
levels of, 24, *27;* model of, 38–39;
model programs to improve, 40–41;
predictor of, 38; self-concept and, 29;
socioeconomic status and, 38
mathematics and science, importance of
background in (for entering labor market), 151
mathematics courses: access to advanced, 41; decisions to enroll in,
23–24; instruction in, *36, 37;* race
and, 30–32, 41; remedial, 25, 26; results of enrollment in advanced, 29;
socioeconomic status and enrollment
in advanced, 38
Mathematics Engineering Science
Achievement (MESA) project, 41
mathematics self-concept, 37–38
Math/Science Workshops Project of Professional Development Program,
118–120
Matzeliger, Jan, 11–12
medical schools, 145–146. *See also*
health professions
mentors and sponsors for black graduate
students, 61, 76
Minnesota Science Assessment and Research Project (SARP), 44, 47–48, 49
Minority Institutions Science Improvement Program (MISIP), 107
minority students, in predominantly
white institutions, 120. *See also*
intervention
Morehouse College, 68, *72–73*

National Assessment of Educational
Progress (NAEP), 25, 27; Computer
Survey of, 39
National Commission on Excellence in
Education, 26
National Council of Teachers of Mathe-
matics, 25
National Science Foundation (NSF) pro-
grams to increase black representation
in quantitative-based careers, 40
Nation at Risk, A, 26
New York Hospital, 16

Nobel laureates, 149
North Carolina A. and T. State Univer-
sity, 71, *72, 73,* 74
Northern California Council of Black
Professional Engineers (NCCBPE), 107

Office of Civil Rights (OCR) Higher Education General Information Survey
(HEGIS), 60, 64–78

parents, 138; needed role of, 139, 144;
Project Interface and, 108, 110, 121
patents granted to free blacks and slaves,
10–11
peer groups, supportive academic, 121
Ph.D. degrees: academic rank and, 93,
95, *96,* 97; black females with,
80–81; blacks attaining, 82–83, 145;
blacks in population with, 79–82;
employment fields and sectors and,
88, 89; employment plans and opportunities and, 84–85; employment
trends and, *87;* funding for study for,
83; most important employer of those
with, 101; primary work activity and,
90, 92–93; salaries and, 97–99, 101;
tenure status and, 93; time to attain,
83; unemployment and underemployment and, 85–88
Ph.D. population, blacks in, 79–82
physical science: bachelors' degrees
from TBIS in, 69, *70, 72,* 74; courses
in, 49, *50;* doctorates from TBIS in,
70, 71, 74; masters' degrees from
TBIS in, 69, *70, 73;* test items in, 57
Polytechnic Institute of New York, *73,*
75
poverty, proportion of blacks born into,
151
Prairie View A. and M. University, *73,*
74
prediction of future events, understanding of scientific theory for, 47
predominantly white institutions (PWIS),
71, 75–76; minority students in, 120
premedical students, Project SOAR and,
111

problem-solving methods, 45, 54, 121; teaching of, 112–113, 115
Professional Development Program (PDP): approach of, 116–117; faculty control of, 120; goal of, 117; graduate program of, 117; high school program of, 117; honors aspect of, 120; informal study groups in, 121; isolation of minority students and, 120–121; main component of, 117; mathematics sequence in, 117–118; pipeline approach and continuity of support and, 120; Special Scholarship Committee of University of California, Berkeley Division, and, 116; staff of, 119; as subject of theses and dissertations, 119; undergraduate program of, 117, 119, 121
professional specialties, blacks as percent of people employed in, 80
Profiles: College-Bound Seniors, 51
Project Interface, 106, 121; awards as motivators and, 108; evaluation of effectiveness of, 109; field trips and, 108; funding for, 107; goals of, 107; junior college students as tutors and role models in, 110–111; measures of success of, 110; parents and, 108, 110; rate of attrition from, 110; relationship with schools, 109; tutorial sessions in, 107
Project SOAR, 121; admission to program, 112; beginnings of, 111; components of program, 112; health professions and, 111, 113–115; high school teachers' participation and training and, 115; laboratory experiments in, 112; methods used in, 112–115; motivation in, 113; Piagetian theory and, 111, 115; problem solving and, 112–113; results of, 114–115; study skills in, 112, 114
psychology: blacks in field of, 80, 81, 82; consulting as primary work of Ph.D.s in, 90, 92
public libraries, blacks denied use of, 18
public school expenditures, 6

quantitative-based careers, programs to increase black representation in, 40
quantitative ideas, black English and, 139
quantitative skills, growing importance of, 150

race: enrollment in type of curriculum and, 29–32; mathematics course enrollment and, *31*
racism, 18; academic, 145; black scientists and, 16–17, 63, 137
reasoning skills, 26
recognition, black scientists' lack of, 16–17
recruitment practices: benefits of, 148; black students and institutional, 63
remedial programs, attitude toward, 120. *See also* intervention
research and development as primary work of Ph.D.s, 90, *92,* 93
research facilities, black access to, 16
research grants, 152
research problems: about blacks, 134; of black sociologists, 133; choice of, 149; culture and choice of, 132–134; selection of, 130–132
research productivity, race and, 147
retired persons, utilization of, 151
Rillieux, Norbert, 11
role models, 61, 141; junior college students as tutors and, 110

St. Paul's College (Lawrenceville, VA), 17
salaries: of black academics, 147; of Ph.D.s, 97–99; of teachers, 4–5
SARP, *see* Minnesota Science Assessment and Research Project (SARP)
SAT, *see* Scholastic Aptitude Test (SAT)
scholarships, 107; organizations contributing to, 151. *See also* financial aid
Scholastic Aptitude Test (SAT): black students' performance on, 62; scores in basic mathematics, 25
school expenditures (1930–31), 4–5, *6*

schools: black attendance, 5; blacks' and immigrants' problems in public, 8; computer access in low-income, 40; corporate adoption of, 151; one-room, 5; segregated, 7, 123; shorter terms for black, 5; structuring science programs in, 57. *See also* classroom processes

schools for blacks, post-Reconstructionist Southern, 4

school structures and processes, societal inequities and, 143

science achievement tests: divergence between attitudes and, 55; enrollment in advanced high school science courses and, 44; physics and chemistry items in, 57; scores in, 43, 51–54

science activities: exposure to, 48; field trips, 108; participation in, 47

science and engineering: attitudes toward, 24, 43, 45, *46*, 47–48, 54, 55, 56, 139; benefits of recruiting blacks into, 136; black female Ph.D.s in, 100; black females in, 145; black Ph.D.s in, 82–83; black underrepresentation in, 60–63; causes and meaning of blacks' response style toward, 48; early exposure to experiences in, 58; educational practices to improve participation and performance in, 56; effects of taking advanced courses in, 142; enrollment and degree attainment in, 64, *65, 66,* 67–69, *70,* 71, *72, 73,* 74–78; experiences related to, 45, 47, 54; factors that discourage black participation in, 63; failure of black high school students to understand methodology of, 55; gender differences in achievement in, 141–142; problem-solving methods in, 45, 54, 121; social funneling into, 126; teaching of, 111–113, 115

science attitudes, 24, 37–38, 43, 45, *46,* 47–48, 54, 56, 138; divergence between achievement scores and, 55

science courses, *see* high school science courses

science enrollment patterns, 48–51, 57, 67–68

science Ph.D.s, field and primary work activity and, *91. See also* advanced degrees; Ph.D. degrees

scientific careers, 10–17; attitudes toward, 47, 48; underrepresentation of blacks in, 51. *See also* career plans and expectations

scientific community, underrepresentation of blacks in, 1

scientific process, awareness of assumptions and methods of, 47

scientists and engineers: in America, 1; blacks as percent of, 80, 126; employment among, 60–61, *127;* field selection among, 128; hostile work environments for minority, 63; minority women as, 61, 68; research problems selected by, 130–132; unemployment of, 146; women as, 125–126. *See also* black scientists

self-confidence in academic abilities, 57

self-help, conditions for, 152

self-image, 107–108

self-taught individuals, 13

sex differences: in enrollment and degree attainment, 68, 76; in mathematics, 141–142

slaves: educational programs for former, 3; inventions by, 10

social change and processes, 123–124

socially constructive activities, engaging in, 48

social sciences, blacks in, 80, 81, *82*

societal inequities, school structures and processes and, 143

societal problems, belief about individual actions to solve, 47

socioeconomic status: influence of, 126; mathematics and, 38

Southern University, 68, *72–73*

standardized tests, 144; black students with high potential but low scores on, 148. *See also* test scores

study skills: deficiencies in, 117; Project SOAR and, 112, 114

Survey of Doctorate Recipients, 79
Survey of Earned Doctorates, 79

talent: distribution of, 125; identifying, 77; wasted, 144
talent pool formation, 148
teachers: attitudes toward, 47; black English and training of, 139–40; computer-literate, 40; expectations and commitment of, 41; influence of, 139; need to enhance training of science, 56; poor science, 58; programs to train mathematics, 40–41
teachers' salaries, 4–5
teaching as primary work of Ph.D.s, 90, 92
teaching style effective with minority students, 58
tenure status of Ph.D.s, 93
test scores, 44, 55; black students with high potential but low, 148; science achievement, 43. *See also* standardized tests
Texas Southern University, 68, *73*
tracking, *30*, 138, 139; determinants of level of, 143; racially segregated classes and, 142; status maintenance and, 143. *See also* curriculum
traditionally black institutions (TBIS), 68–69, *70*, 71, *72–74*, 74–78, 144–145; partnerships between research universities, industry, and government laboratories and, 152; proportionate share of scientific and technical talent, 143
transportation for black schoolchildren, 5, 20
Turner, Charles H., 16, 18
Tuskegee Institute, 9, 14, 68
tutorial programs for minorities: in graduate and professional schools, 63; Project Interface and, 106–111

tutors, junior college students as, 107, 109–110

unemployment, among scientists and technically trained persons, 146
United States Office of Education, 44
University of California at Berkeley, 116
University of Chicago, 15, 16
University of the District of Columbia, *72*, 74
University of Illinois, Urbana, *74*, 75
University of Massachusetts, Amherst, *74*, 75
University of Vienna, 15
Upward Bound Program, 116

vocabulary building, 113
vocational education, 9, 14. *See also* industrial education
volunteers: in intervention programs, 151; Project Interface and, 108

Washington, Booker T., 9, 14
West Virginia State College, 15
Whimbey, Arthur, 115
white academic institutions, *see* predominantly white institutions (PWIS)
white high schools: mathematics achievement and, 33–34; mathematics instruction in predominantly black and, *36*
Why Johnny Can't Add, 25
women in science, 125–126. *See also* black females; sex differences
Woods, Granville T., 11, 12
work environments, hostile, 63
Wright, Louis Tompkins, 16

Xavier University (New Orleans), 111

Yale University, 13–14